The A–Qu

the search for authenticity and connection

discovering ourselves one question at a time

Alan Gratias

This journey is dedicated to those who struggle to live their everyday wisdom

Alan Gratias is the founder and creator of the *Gravitatis* brand, including the entertainment *Gravitas – the game that gets us thinking and talking again.* As the original Gravitarg, he works with people from all neighborhoods and cultures to bring out their inner wisdom. He pioneered the concept of Gravitas Quotient as a factor in the determination of how individuals make out in life, and the notion of a Life Puzzle that has to be decoded individual by individual. He lives on a restored Loyalist farm at the water's edge on an island county in Ontario where he tends to his chardonnay, lavender, and ongoing deterioration.

The Authentic Self – solving our Life Puzzle

Life is all about working out who we are, and who we are can change over time depending on where we have been. The secret to solving our Life Puzzle is to build and decode what I call our ENA – our Experiential Neural Access. So it is not only about our DNA that imprint us at birth, but about how we learn from our experiences and environments and incorporate that learning into our behavior. We want to be able to show the triumph of what might be called ordinary, personal, or everyday wisdom.

We are overdue for a correction to the national obsession with social networking. *With all our communications gadgets, we are coming so much closer to never having to talk to anyone again. There seems to be a universal hunger for connection and emotional synchronicity.*

The A- Quest is a compendium of questions and notes to a series of intriguing questions, some profound, some personal, some amusing, about the lessons individuals have learned that have deepened their understanding of what the French call 'la condition humaine'.

Being 'real' is increasingly revered in a world that yearns for transparency and admires self-disclosure. Social networking sites are designed to encourage shallow interactions but in an Age of Confession, *The A-Quest* plays to the search to find meaning, connection and wisdom in our individual stories. The search for wisdom is no different from the search for any talent - *we are often surprised where we find it.* We can go into every neighbourhood, community and culture to find individuals with ordinary wisdom.

We live one experience, and then another, and another. Learning along the way, we become the sum of our experiences. Long before the founding of Rome, the Etruscans measured time by something called 'saeculum' which spanned from a given moment until the last people who had lived through that moment had died. Saeculum is the extent of hard memory for human events and a certain kind of loss, the moment when lessons cannot be captured for the record.

You can tell whether a person is clever by their answers. You can tell whether a person is wise by their questions. A wise man will not proselytize you. If you are willing, he may guide you to find your own answers. A wise person will not try to convince you of anything. A wise person will share what they know, but you have to ask. They have their quest. They assume you have yours.

Gravitas Quotient

Gravitas Quotient is a measure of one's reserves of inner wisdom. It is a measure of our individual ENA. GQ is all about how we learn and grow from our experiences. It is the distillation of what we believe about life, ourselves and the world around us.

Gravitas Quotient is the Third Dimension, the 3D of our intelligence. It represents the depth of our awareness of what goes on around us. Ultimately our GQ determines how much fulfillment we get out of life. The human software is make of up of three components, Intelligence Quotient (IQ), Emotional Quotient (EG) and Gravitas Quotient (GQ) . Gravitas Quotient can be expressed as IQ + EQ + A-Quest = GQ

If we can hypothesize there are discrete stages in life, for example, birth, childhood, adolescence, adulthood, there is one that is ignored, the one most tied to a sense of an individual's fulfillment. The Gravitatis Threshold (GT) is the point at which our interior authenticity is converted to living wisdom and becomes a guide of conduct.

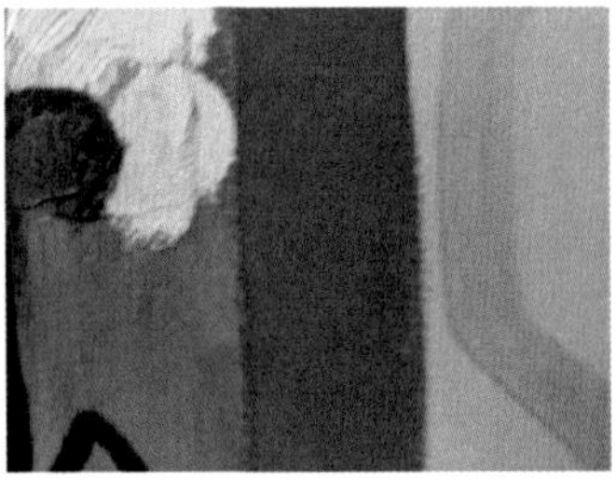

Discovering ourselves - the millennial party

New Year's Eve, 1999 was a momentous occasion, the only time any of us would see a new century. Looking back, it is easy to forget how consequential the turning of the millennium seemed. The dire predictions about the collapse of cyberspace and other cataclysmic events took hostage of our mindsets as the world approached the end of 1999. Joanie and I took a ride on the waves of hysteria and euphoria.

We went back and forth on the best way to celebrate. We wanted to make an effort to say farewell to the second millennium but with a new dog in residence, we wanted to stay close to home. With only a few weeks left before the year 2000 took hold, Roger had established herself as a noisy and ubiquitous member of the household. Because the kitchen and dining room at Cressy House, our crumbling country retreat, had advanced from shambles to functionality, we stuck to a tried and true formula.

We decided to host a dinner party for twelve, a Last Supper of the century, half from the city who could be housed in our unfinished Longhouse. The out-of-towners included my old amigos Bob, Len and Gordon from Toronto, Tim and his new fiancé, Simone, and Peter and Jennifer who had recently met each other in my make- shift kitchen. The others, David and Karen, John and Margaret, were neighbours on County Road 8.

The anticipation of an elegant sit-down dinner for twelve was punctured by the call from Deo. Joanie was dead set against adding my twin brother to the mix. She knew how the dynamics would change.

"There are too many collisions when he is around. He's a holding pen waiting to be released," Joanie argued. "Just say no."

D had a ready counter to my pleas there was no room at the inn.

"I'll bring an air mattress. Sally and I will sleep in the library." Sally Venn was his newest in-between-wives-girlfriend. "Bro, we have to bring in the third millennium together."

We needed a focus to capture the spirit of the double ritual of bidding farewell to one era and welcoming another. I took Roger for a walk along the ridge to think about what we might do. Half way up the escarpment, I had my eureka moment.

"A memory capsule! Everyone will leave something behind in a buried container."

Roger must have liked the idea because she bounded back across the snow from her lead position. She sat at my feet giving me 'the stare' that is at the heart of the dog/man bond. The memory riddance game could keep our group engaged until the champagne was uncorked and the fireworks launched.

I asked each guest to bring one item of significance that they wanted to bury at midnight. I left it ambiguous whether the item was something they wished to shed, or a token of the life they had happily lived. Roger had determined where the burial hole should be located. Her favourite hiding spot for her bones was in the field between the house and the vineyard under the Baby Walnut tree. We prepared a hole three feet deep so that at midnight the revelers could stand around the lip and take turns shoveling topsoil to inter their artifacts.

I hadn't thought about what would happen to the capsule. My intention was to create an activity to encourage my friends to talk about their lives over good food, sympathetic company, and lashes of wine and champagne.

The joviality started building with the arrival of the first guests in mid-afternoon. Deo and Sally ensconced themselves in the library, lit the fire, and started to ramp up. Bro's manic energy unzipped the camaraderie earlier than expected. As the others arrived, there was no sense of holding back. Joanie and I had counted on some downtime before unfurling the flag, but the party was on, Deo front and center, black tie and tails swirling around the unfinished rooms of Cressy House.

"Can he keep going?" Joanie asked me as the last guests, Tim and Simone, settled in at six o'clock. "Or is it junk energy that will peak too early?"

I nodded in the direction of the bar where Deo was mixing drinks in tall glasses.

"He will carry the load until the appointed hour and then he'll crash and burn," I counseled sotto voce.

"The best martinis north of Manhattan," purred Sally.
"Not martinis, my dear, I am building Negronis – rye, and quantro," D announced. "The Italian cocktail."
"It is supposed to ber gin, Campari and sweet vermouth," I corrected, attempting to dislodge Bro from his pedestal.
"My version loosens tongues faster," Deo said offering a highball glass to Sally.
Well into dinner with the candles burning down and the conversations lubricating, I rose at the head of the table. "I have asked each one of you to bring a personal memento to leave behind in a Memory Capsule"
"I'll go first," Tim Wilson interrupted, "on the principle, it's better to get it out of the way."
He stepped over Roger and walked to the crackling fire. Shadows crisscrossed his face like a harlequin dancing off stage. He reached into his pocket and pulled out a burnished gold waistcoat watch.
"My grandfather gave me this timepiece when I turned eighteen. He was a father figure to me because I hardly knew my own Dad who died when I was five."
Tim fielded a torrent of queries with great candor. A friend of twenty years revealed a persona we had not known. We saw him with fresh eyes. He became vulnerable, garrulous and authentic. Tim stepped onto the raised hearth and dropped the antique Waltham into the canister. The clang jolted Roger from her watchfulness and us from our revelry. We were in momentary shock that Tim had actually disposed of the keepsake. He stepped down from the hearth, and we all stood up and cheered.
That set the stage for Bob who put away the first lock of hair his mother had cut from his Vikingish red hair. Len deposited his father's doctored passport which enabled him to become a holocaust survivor. Simone plunked a vinyl LP of Eddy Duchin her mother played endlessly dealing with the grief of losing her husband. David dropped a grade school report which observed on his disruptive behaviour in the classroom.
A barrage of questions followed each drop. In a free-for-all interrogation, we called out our personal questions. "What was the most valuable lesson you learned from your parents." "What's good about growing up in dysfunctional family?" "What question would you most like to have answered?" Everyone was prepared to reveal a vulnerability.

Roger lay by the fire, ears pinched forward like Cerebus guarding the Gates of Veritas. Each time a guest dropped an item in the canister, she barked furiously until the tin stopped reverberating. I tossed in a draft of a fantasy novel I had written, 'The Kingsburg Elixir' along with dozens of rejection letters from agents and publishers.
Deo jumped onto the raised bricks to keep the momentum going. At forty-four his face still unlined, his hair shaggy in a teen idol sort of way, an improbable beauty. He had a vellum sheet of paper in hand. He began to read.

" If only I had loved her/ like I could have loved her/ she'd be here beside me/ through the cold and windy night
I whispered secret feelings/ through salty sated lips/Now those secret feelings/ are emptied in the night
I would make for her a garden/ to burst in endless bloom /a thousand white lilies/ and freesia for her bed"

D was interrupted with a barrage of questions. Who was she? What went wrong? Isn't she better off without you? He danced and weaved in his responses, ducking and diving with humour and élan.
A disbelief settled on the guests like confetti at a wake, before Gordon cried out, "put your regrets in the bin Casanova."
Bob liked to goat my twin, having been caught as collateral damage in some of his earlier train wrecks. He called out, "What do you wish your mother understood about you?"
The singularity of the question silenced the room. Everyone was working out their own answer. For once D did not rip off a facile retort.
"I wish Betty understood that just because I was born a few minutes before my twin, does not make me a superior person."
Then he turned the question on each of us with a caveat.
"Memory is subjective, which makes the truth elusive. Don't tailor your past in an effort to reshape your lives."
I flinched knowing how Bro himself had sliced and diced his past to order to create a self he could live with.
"Isn't it easier to make fiction than reveal reality," Tim called out.
"Fiction and fact are so intertwined, what's the point of making a distinction," David added.

On his way back to his seat Deo did a little jig, somewhere between Chubby Checker and Michael Jackson, all gyrating legs and undulating pelvis which in any other company, would have been interpreted as a mating dance. But here on this grand occasion at the turn of an epoch, the wagging head and syncopating shoulders got tabbed as D's 'regretti jive'.
We became so engrossed in our exposes of our mother relationships that we almost lost the moment. Just in time I herded everyone outside for the midnight countdown being announced on the radio.
I had purchased two dozen rockets from the Mohawks on the Tyendinaga Reserve to set off at the stroke of midnight. The fireworks were set in a line of buckets on the shoreline. The young Tansley boy, my next door neighbour's son, ran from pail to pail igniting each bundle of fireworks in a freeform of flash and thunder.
Somewhere about one am I led a procession to the burial ground under the Baby Walnut Tree guiding a wheelbarrow carrying our Memory Capsule. Fourteen of us stood vigil as I secured the lid, and together we lowered the canister into the hole.
We took turns shoveling dirt over our vault of disposed treasures.
Shoulder to shoulder, we bade farewell to a slice of our memory banks.
Leonard spoke a Yiddish prayer in remembrance of times past, and things put away

they showed a lot of gravitas

Bob and Gordon stayed up in the Longhouse past four in the morning. When Gordon gets going, he is hard to stop. He is one of those sorts whose resting disposition is quiet and introverted, but when fueled by the grape and presented with a new audience, a funny gene is liberated. Bob goes in the opposite direction. He is naturally articulate and voluble but as wine consumption increases, he becomes quieter. The two are made for each on binges. Reports are that Gordon worked his accents of the world as the imaginary Speaker of a United Nations parliament. Collison giggled endlessly.

They both missed the debrief over coffee the next day.

The disposal of memories in the canister had brought everyone closer. We felt more connected to each other in shared epiphanies.

"There is something deliberately distorting about memory," Deo mused on the previous evening's drama.
"Perhaps what we remember never happened at all," Sally said.
"More like a story made up of something in the past." I continued. "Is that what you were trying to do D? Distort the facts of a painful memory."
"Memory is its own breed of fiction," D pressed on. "We can lose it and we can create it."
"I hope you are a reliable narrator of your own story Bro because you must remember I was there," I interjected.
"You can distort the facts but never the feeling," Tim countered.
He was the one who got us started. "To Tim," I said raising my mug to Tim and Simone snuggled together on the step between the kitchen and the dining room. "The piper who showed the way."
Len, the Ph'd in Social Policy, jumped in definitively. "We believe our memories to be true. We don't consciously invent them."
"Self-curate or disappear," D added mischievously. "We should document our lives." Deo, my sibling who might have uttered the line about history being that certainty produced at the point where the imperfections of memory meet the inadequacies of documentation.

Roger swiveled her head at each contribution, fixing her hypnotic gaze on each emerging philosopher.

I couldn't resist another ping at Dag, the inveterate chronicler of his own life. "For some people memory is more imagination. They remember things the way they wished them to have been."
D shot back. "And we lead a happier life." Then lowering his voice in a way that combined shyness and authority he added, "the only things that count are the things we remember."
"Let's dig up the capsule next year and deposit more memories," Joanie suggested.
"I've had enough honesty," Bob deferred. "I want to put my mask back on."
"You speak in probes Alan," David complained to me. I
"Your brain," Deo intervened, "feels like a trapeze artist jumping from idea to idea." He looked at the others for affirmation. "Sometimes you become too meta."
Sure D. That will flummox everyone. I was not going to allow the conversation to end on that zinger.

"And you Dag, excel at playing the shaman."
"Facts," he shot back, "are the building blocks of myth."

Throughout the day, we regrouped around a game of boules in the snow and a ski through the vineyard. We revisited the previous evening's confessions, exploring a range of interpretations.
"Better than a session with a shrink," Len cracked.
"Better than chocolate," chimed in Simone.
Over the following weeks I was ambushed by snippets of revelations, and visual fragments of figures standing on a crackling fire hearth, searching for the authenticity of their lives. My eureka moment came in late January of the new millennium on a hike with Deo and Roger around the perimeter of the farm. Deo was asking about any large tract of land that might be available for purchase.

We stopped to absorb the brilliant sunshine on the fresh snow that transformed Cressy House to a pristine mirage. Roger bounded in circles around us. Deo put a hand on my shoulder.

"Maybe we should convert your place to a retreat for wise people like Tim and Bob and Len. They showed a lot of gravitas. They brought out the innate wisdom in others."
"In the end the only wisdom we acquire is humility," I said.
D took off his sunglasses and pinched his grip on my arm. His high nose glistened in the sun.
"You should do something with your questions and answers Mr. Socrates. *It's a strip tease of the mind.*"
"I'm not sure. The evening was an exception," I replied. "Most people enjoy skimming the surface."
"Surface is all many of us will ever have," Deo countered. "I can't think of anything more exciting than the surface of things."

I stared at Deo, wavering whether to challenge him.
"You enjoy the theatre of the mind too much," I said. "To be authentic, you have to speak the truth."

"The self is a perpetually rewritten story," Deo replied.

what's your GQ?

"Wisdom is putting experience in context." Bro was in a contemplative mode.

Hell that's all I wanted him to do. Look at the context of his own mother living in a state of severe dementia, and start taking some responsibility. Couldn't he take over for a few weeks just to give me a break?

D was on the phone doing his weekly check on Mum, not wanting to talk to her, just ensuring I was well strapped into the mother-care harness. He could care less about her well-being. These days all he wanted to chat about the idea of Gravitas. Our Millennium Cannister Caper had lit up some previously inert neurons. He seemed to think because 'gratias' and 'gravitas' both had Latin roots, that he should become a prophet for reinventing ancient wisdoms.

D was like a rat trapped in cheese when he gobbed onto a line of enquiry. "Gravitas is an essential building block on the journey toward fulfillment," he chortled down the line. "It makes us the subject of our own lives."

"And you more than anyone," I countered, "need to grow from your experiences. It is what intelligent life is all about."

I rang off knowing he would ring call back the next day conjuring up further bons mots on the subject. The phone jangled before 7 am.

Deo was bursting with insights that he had no hope of actualizing.

"I have figured it out. The human software consists of three elements. IQ and EQ we know about. But it is the third element, the elusive Gravitas Quotient, which is a measure of our reserves of wisdom."

"D that's the point about the game," I said. "It distills what we believe about life."

"It's more than that," Deo exclaimed. "It represents the Third Dimension, the 3D of our intelligence. Gravitas Quotient represents the *depth* of our awareness of what goes on around us."

"That's quite an insight, D," I taunted. "What's your GQ?"

*

After five years of living with me and the round the clock care program I had cobbled together, Mother had reached a stage of panic. She needed to see or touch someone every few minutes to validate her existence. The comfort of living with her son in the neighbourhood she had grown up was lost. Overnight, she become incontinent and gave up walking.

Matte and Mohammed, her principal caregivers, and I bundled Betty up for the short journey to her new home in late 2003. We were nervous about her reaction to the cloistered shelter of the Alzheimers unit on the eighth floor. The Glebe Centre was a twelve storey nursing home on Bank Avenue opposite Lansdowne Park, the principal event stadium in downtown Ottawa. Mother enjoyed the fuss being made over her arrival, and the opportunity to flirt with the dark-skinned male nurses. For a brief period, she returned to her favourite role of party doll.

She didn't miss a beat in settling into her new digs, a room with a few of her furnishings and photos overlooking the playing field on the other side of street.

We bid adieu to Mother that afternoon at she lay down for a nap.

"Darling," she purred from the hospital bed, "I love your new house."

Elizabeth Constance Plaunt Gratias lived in The Glebe Center for a year before passing away in her sleep in her 89th year. Mother died January 28 of that year, 2004, the year I launched Gravitas – *the game that gets us thinking and talking again*. I gave some of her ashes to Anna and prepared to bury the remainder in a metal box beside Valdo. Deo would have nothing to do with the ceremony I had planned for the occasion.

"You always wanted her for yourself," he said from Cloudy Bay Farm in Nova Scotia, dismissing my plea to join Anna and I for the ritual. "Now you deal with her soul."

"Just a breach of eternity," I replied in full gravitas mode. "Our time on earth is an imaginary half-nothing."

"When my parenthesis ends," he replied. "I want you, Alan, to provide my life with a narrative."

"You want *me* to give *your* life meaning," I said. "That's a charge for a superhero."

*

Anna and I, Joanie and Roger buried Mother's ashes next to Valdo's urn at the foot of the dry-stone wall enclosing the loggia, husband and wife lying intertwined with the roots of the wisteria tree. That corner of the stone wall is the point where the views of the orchard, the water, the vineyard and the lavender merge in a scintillating outlook of possibility.

We bid adieu to Mum with a champagne toast.

"Will the misfits find peace?" Anna asked.

"Or their survivors?" I added.

With the passing of our parents, and the move to the familial front ranks for the three of us, something fractured in Deo. The ligature tying him to convention snapped. The brother who had so surely walked the tightrope of modality, fell off. Deo set out to test new boundaries. He no longer cared about family opinion. Sally Venn was the first to be caught in his cross-hairs. And I became his instrument of her entrapment.

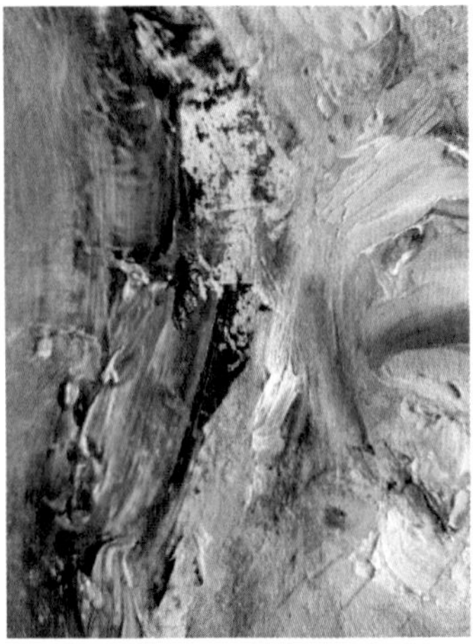

she's a wisdom whisperer

I do admit it was Deo who got me thinking about how individuals express the truth of their lives. Why some people integrate experiences better than others. I became engaged in the conundrum of how people reveal who they really are, rather than who they appear to be.
With the help of Roger, Joanie and many dinner guests over the subsequent months in 2001 and 2002, I put together a box of questions cards. Some profound, some personal and some quirky, all the questions were designed to illicit answers about how individuals have lived their lives, and how they saw their relationship to the world. The idea was to have fun, not to negotiate a hand-wringing, gut wrenching inquisition. The intention was to gently probe what people understood of what the French call 'la condition humaine', to unpack their interior wisdoms.
I say 'with the help of Roger' because she became a sort of arbiter at these noisy dinner parties. Over the years she had become adept at spotting liars and sociopaths. She outed my contractor-carpenter who was cheating me five ways to Sunday and saved me from the purchase of a hotel after finding the debris of a fire in the stairwell. She nosed out Dag's machinations before I did. She thought everything he did smelled of ferret.

To that repertoire of skills, Roger now added 'truth-finder'. When the Rubbermaid menu-card holder came out at the cheese course, she assumed a sitting position beside me. Her eyes and ears followed each question and the round table of answers. My entertainment product had evolved to the point of seventy 3 x 5 inch cards each with three questions. The first was meant to be serious ('give an example of a universal truth'), the second personal ('how do you express adoration?). The third question was humorous or open-ended like 'what should have happened' or 'what are the attributes of a great hug'. These are meant to be questions you have not been asked before. The answers can be heartfelt, witty or even flippant. If a response speaks to the Enquirer, whose receptivity changes after a verre or two, that person gets the card and wins the round. Of course the entertainment is not about winning but engaging each other.

Let's face it, no one wants to be duped. We want the real deal. We want truth and the revelation of self. There is something fascinating about the private world of others. There is something hard core about authenticity that strikes deep. 'Uthenticitey' is what I call it – the willingness to make yourself the subject of your own life.

In theory the first person to accumulate three cards wins, but no one plays by the rules. No one cares who wins. We want to connect with other people, hear their stories and understand how they have evolved to who they are. Roger can detect the most honest answer, which may not be the winning answer, although sincerity usually trumps wit. Roger knows the human face is a moving landscape of tremendous nuance and complexity. There is something about body language, the modulation of the voice, and the scent of veracity that sends Roger from my side to lie at the foot of the most genuine answerer.

If dogs can detect cancer, mold, and epileptic seizures in humans, is it far-fetched to assert that Roger can track authenticity? With their superior olfactory equipment, 220 million smell-sensitive cells over an area the size of a pocket handkerchief compared to 5 million cells over the size of a postage stamp for humans, dogs can sniff out blood sugar levels with 90 % accuracy. Dogs can detect sounds as low as the 16 to 20 Hz range, compared to 20-70 Hz for humans and as high as 100,00 hz, compared to 20,000 Hz for humans. Their ears have a degree of mobility that pinpoints the exact location of a sound. Eighteen muscles tilt, rotate, and raise a dog's ear. When you combine their hearing and smelling capacities, dogs become phenoms at observing human behaviour.

Take Exhibit A, my octogenarian neighbour Gerry, who sits at the dining room table with the hang dog look of the retired Anglican Minister he is. He is contemplating the enquiry 'what question would you most like to have answered?' He sighs before responding in a measured enunciation.
"The question I would most like to have answered is when is my raging carnal appetite going to diminish?". There is scent and temperature in his phrases as much as there are words. Gerry's bodily calibrations run amok to the course of his words. Chemicals, and proteins and fluids don't lie. This response is genuine. Roger feels the heat and glow. She gets up from my side to lie at Gerry's feet.
"That dog is a damn truth-whisperer" Dag muttered as Gerry is awarded the winning card.

the game that gets us thinking and talking again

I called my beta entertainment 'Gravitas'. My friends labelled it 'The Little Box of Big Questions' or 'Soc's Box', Socrates being Deo's tag line for my enquiring ways. I have always liked the way the word gravitas rolls off the tongue. A Latin word denoting weight or substance, it growls at you and looks you straight in the eye. Over time the word has become adopted by the English language referring to a quality of an individual with a depth of personality and seriousness of purpose. In classical Rome, 'gravitas' was one of the four virtues necessary for a person of respect – the others being 'pietas', 'dignitas', and 'iustitia'. In my books gravitas is an essential building block of the human journey toward fulfillment.

We can aspire to have gravitas, but can it be acquired? Or is it simply part of our DNA? Joanie has it in spades, Roger too and Deo shows decent deposits. In the first few years of the third millennium, at dozens of occasions at the farm, guests, friends, and drop-ins demonstrated great reserves of insight and savoir faire when I jumped in front of them with a spontaneous question from the box. I concluded that virtually everyone has natural gravitas if they are willing to plumb their depths. It is as simple, and complex as learning and growing from our experiences - the essence of an intelligent life.

So 'Gravitas' the game became part of our social life at Cressy House. Lest you think this a earnest household, keep in mind that wit and humour usually won the day. Joanie and I were constantly testing new questions on each other. I shout to her harvesting the lavender, 'who is the stranger at the door? She replies "Deo and I wish he would go away." Then counters "who do you wish would call you?" To which I reply "The Family Institute confirming Deo has been decertified as a twin."

a strip tease of the mind

"What makes a good question?" Deo mused as he Joanie and I walked up and down the rows of the vineyard inspecting for signs of botrytis on the grapes. Roger led the way with her nose. She could smell the sweetness of the rot before we could see it. The prolonged wet spring of 2003 gave rise to conditions of grey rot, a fungus that infects grape bunches.

"The first criteria for a good question is that it is unusual, one that you have not been asked before," I replied, kneeling to examine the punky skin of a grape bunch Roger had led us to. I could see mould spores spreading across the surface of the grapes.

"The second is that it allows a wide range of responses. The question should have layers, nuances and ambiguity."

"A gravitas question can be interpreted on a number of levels," Joanie added.

"I get it," Deo said. "Good questions allow you to jelly down on your core. Really unpack and probe."

I handed the rotting grapes to Deo.

"Let's use these grapes as an example. They have a fungus that accelerates deterioration, I observed dropping the bunch on the ground.

"Why do organisms deteriorate is not a good question, but 'when is deterioration a positive force' is," I continued.

D threw me the 'do say old chappie' look.

I pressed on with my example.

"Botrytis can also give rise to noble rot, or what the French call 'la pourriture noble'. This occurs when the grape are exposed to drier conditions and become partially raisined. At a certain point the grapes produce a concentrated sweet wine such as Sauternes."

I swaggered at my viticultural trump card.

D squished the grapes with twist of his Bluntstone boot. "That's like lauding a low dose of poison."

"Dangerous substances can be beneficial at low levels," I said. "At a certain exposure, the relationship changes from toxic to therapeutic."

"Does that mean that DDT can prevent cancer instead of causing it?" Deo asked.

"The principle is that all things can be both beneficial and poisonous."
"You mean a little bit of me goes a long way," D asked.
"You are like a dose of botox," Joanie replied. "A single needle last many months.'"
Deo stayed at Cressy House for a few more days before decamping back to Westmount and his shenanigans with Sally Venn, his accomplice in the master plan to swindle Waupoos Island out from under the Oblates. He liked my definition of a robust question, offering up dozens of examples which met the standard. He hijacked me at all hours of the day and night to toss out a potential enquiry.
"What is the best way to deal with unrequited love?"
"What is your most delicious fetish?"
"Why should we pause on the threshold?"
"What is good about surrender?"
"How do you get rid of a lover?"
Gravitas questions were an intrigue to him. A way of working out his own world view. A search for moral apercus. By the time he pointed his sleek roadster in the direction of Montreal, the three of us had tested hundreds of probes for the expanding menu box.
"Take it to the market," Deo urged, "Its a strip tease of the mind."
"That's not wisdom," I countered, "that's the conceit of wisdom."
He pulled out his wallet, in his classic bravado way. "I'll put skin into the game." He made a gesture to hand me his platinum American Express card.
"Verities can be translated to gold," he purred with an enigmatic air.
We stood behind his car, a Jaguar XE greener than a polished emerald, to make sure he actually left. I pushed on the fender with the encouragement "time to bid adieu"
"Who's riding in your sidecar?" Joanie barked at D in a final volley of our testing stratagem.
He cut the engine and turned to us.
"Have you forgotten? I used to have a Ural Patrol motorcycle. And you, Bro, were always in my sidecar with googles, a leather helmet, and wind in your mouth."
He saluted out the window with a regal flick of his wrist and sped to the end of the lane. He should have turned left on County Road 8 in the direction of the ferry to Kingston, but he turned right. He wanted me to know he had one more stop.

*

“We never done anything like this,” Bob Hambly hesitated. “I like the concept of a game that gets us thinking and talking again.”
He and I, and his wife, Barb Woolley, were sitting in the boardroom of their firm HamblyWoolley whose client list read like a blue blood roster of retailers and cultural institutions. My menu box lay on the table with hundreds of 3 x5 question cards scattered about. All around us cranes swirled to erect condos and hotels in the Bathurst and Wellington core of the west end of Toronto. Mid-way through my pitch, a short haired pointer ambled into the boardroom and collapsed at my feet. Then a second dog, a grizzled Beagle, joined the pointer under the table.
“Libby and Otis sometimes join us,” Bob joked by way of explanation. “They carry out due diligence on new clients.”
I felt a kinship being formed. I had approached the boutique design company on the recommendation of my neighbour in the County, Petra Cooper. She had engaged HamblyWoolley to create the brand of Fifth Town, an artisan goat and sheep cheese start-up she was building half a mile down the road. HW had an excellent reputation as design thinkers and developers. And they listened well. After a ninety- minute session, I had my team to take Gravitas to the market and they had their first game product.
“One further consideration,” I said on the way out. “Can my counsel Roger join me for our next session?”

*

Joanie and I spend hundreds of hours in the summer of 2007 working on the design aspects of the final product. We prototyped dozens of boxes, fonts, and colours before settling on small box with a fitted orange top over a blue base. Inside there were 143 cards about the size of tarot cards with 429 questions, three per card, some profound, some personal and some just piquant, all probing an understanding of what the French call ‘la condition humaine’. Each card was a unique graphic with fragments of the letters G.R.A.V.I.T.A.S. spread over eight colour fields. Putting the cards together in a haphazard jigsaw, an abstract emerged that would not look out of place at the MOMA.

We launched a game of enquiry to discover who we really are, and how we have lived. By trading insights, wisdoms and savoir faire, Gravitas took us away from our smart phones, iPods and reality shows, to connect with real people in real time. More like profound pursuits that Trivial Pursuits, there were no right or wrong answers, just honest, funny and heartfelt ones. In the end Gravitas had no board, no dice and no tokens, just you, and your take on life. Our new mantra became 'unplug and discover the authentic self.'

The entrepreneurial journey made for a bumpy ride. For these novices, the road from idea to production to sales was full of pot holes. We gave birth to 5000 game units in September of 2007. My plan was to use Toronto as a test market to discover the best way to market and retail the product and then expand to similar urban concentrations, the principle being what worked in a sophisticated cosmopolitan market like Toronto should work in other cities in North America. Hands on became my modus operandi and the cold call my specialty. After weeks of pitching strangers about the merits of being confessional about life, I secured a number of orders which included some big retail chains, smaller gift boutiques and book stores.

Demographics can be deceiving. In developing Gravitas, the idea was to appeal to the huge wave of boomers, the pig in the python, the leading edge of whom were reaching sixty-five. But the profile of the actual end user turned out to be younger and hipper. The typical Gravitas buyer was a woman with a college degree 25-40. Younger cohorts snapped up the entertainment because it made them feel more adult. Turned out that kids were more open and confessional than my ageing boomers.

On the weekends at Cressy, resting from our marketing blitz, Joannie and I become giddy at the constant stream of emergency calls for reorders. Roger, not knowing how to handle our delirium, took to hiding the original menu box around the property. The first time it disappeared from its home on the dining room buffet, Joanie and I turned the house upside down, slightly panicked at the loss of our beta version. A few days later I spotted the blue Rubbermaid container protruding from one of Roger's favourite storage vaults at the base of the walnut tree. I dug it out, leaving intact her stash of kibble and hard biscuits. Thereafter when the small blue box went missing, we scoured all her known food deposits.

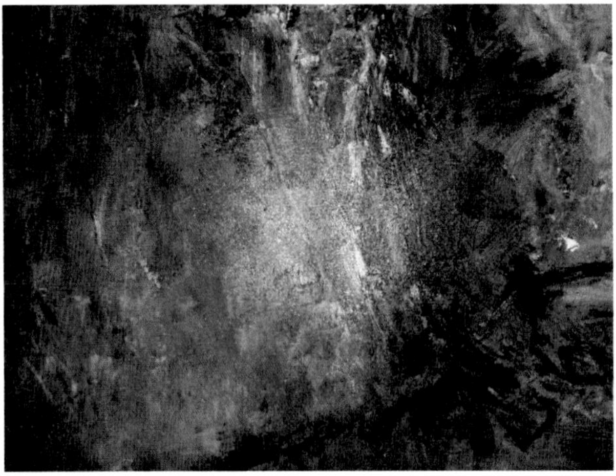

you are superhero material

My twin brother was calling me a 'truth whisperer' as if I was in the business of becalming the feral cognoscenti. He conferred on me Roger's moniker. Now Roger and I were both truth whisperers. I understood a horse whisperer, maybe a dog whisperer, but a truth whisperer, taming truth speakers, was a new one for me. Deo was always persuading me to undertake journeys I did not want to make. He took a perverse pleasure in pushing me to the brink to see if I would take flight.

"You have powers," Deo maintained. "You coax out the authentic self". D was either in charm overdrive or in serious need of therapy. He wanted me to venture into the most unsavoury neighbourhoods of the world in search of universal truths.

"Your questions are shorthand versions of the human experience," he insisted.

"Sounds like you want me to hobble around mean streets looking for peasants to invite for tea," I answered.

"We *must* preserve deposits of wisdom," Deo added in an omniscient manner as if he knew about the future of the world.

We paused at the end of a vineyard row high in a green canopy.

"Don't you feel that IQ tests are not what they are cracked up to be?" Deo asked as he inspected a cluster of grapes.
"People can be smart in so many ways," he continued. "Your questions probe another sort of intelligence."
He leaned into me. "They translate life experiences into authenticity."
"I suppose Gravitas Quotient is a measure of interior wisdom," I responded.
"Go like a wandering monk," Deo continued his refrain, "to find real people in real time who have a singular take on the human condition."
No, I thought. I am content with my life at Cressy House looking after my chardonnay vineyard and field of lavender. Joanie and I, with Roger as our head of security, have created a good life in our adopted home in Prince Edward County. Crumbling houses are my obsessions not the pursuit of everyday truths.
But because it is in the nature of twinship to want to accommodate the other half, I played along with Deo's fancy of launching a superhero. This is what twins do, indulge each other's fantasies. Saitarg was to be my moniker - my name spelled backwards, 'sait' he knows, and 'arg' for argonaut, explorer of unknown places.
We were sitting on the portico of the Longhouse overlooking the tenth largest fresh water lake in the world. The view was more Mediterranean than Canadian Shield. I opened a bottle of our 2010 chardonnay.
"Your chardonnay is the world's best," Deo declared, "without a Burgundy postal code."
"Do you really believe that everyone has the potential to be a superhero," I asked my brother beside me in an Adirondack chair trying to dial down the charm offensive.
"Ordinary people are capable of extraordinary feats in the right circumstance," he replied breaking his trance of contemplation.
"You have a zeal to discover connections and when you do, I have seen how you experience a kind of thrill, like a bumping of souls."
"You are a crazy dreamer D."
"Now is the time to break out your inner self," he cajoled in retaliation to my protest that I like the life we had created at Cressy House. "You are a late bloomer."
"Where does all this come from Bro? You inhabit so many masks," I asked, still incredulous of his repurposing of my life. "You are a banker. You collect women and wives like I collect crumbling houses."

"I was the one born in the caul" he reminded me, as he often does, ignoring reference to his disheveled amours. "The fetus membrane gave *me* the genes of psychotelepathy."

"A toast to the preservation of sagacity," I joked in tribute to our charade.

"You, maestro, have to take it from here", he said as we crossed to the main house, his arm locked in mine. "The planet is ill. Your mission is to save treasures of enlightenment."

Deo returned to Montreal the next day in a cloud of Jaguar- spitting dust to resume the trickery and dashing presence that kept him vibrating in the city. The vendange is a few weeks only. I have to focus on vineyard protection from predators who see the ripening grapes as a food source. As consumed as I am with protecting our crop of chardonnay until full veraison, the notion of Saitarg's quest never abandons my mind.

A wisdom warrior?

But I don't trust Deo. I always suspect my twin's motives, self-absorption and greed being his default instincts. Why does he want to send me to the far reaches of the world in a pursuit of illusory magi? Why the urgency to find these savants, ordinary and originals at the same time, who inhabit a world of authenticity?

He is always saying our planet is sick? Does Deo's psychotelepathy extend to predicting an apocalyptic event? We know there are nightmare scenarios out there, volcanic eruptions, toxic clouds and tipping points galore. But humankind may not need cosmic forces to destroy Mother Earth. Nuclear war, global warming, or a disease pandemic could be the Armageddon. Deo is so beguiling. Somehow he can make the slightest remark sound oracular. Comatose truths crackle to life.

"We're on this planet a short time. Our decisions matter," he says "We have to get our paragraph right."

"Your imagination has gone unruly," I said, "with fiendish ingenuity."

*

"Joanie, maybe there is something to it?"

"To what?"

"Deo's notion of a quest."

We were sitting on the front verandah after a quick tour of the vineyard, taking our evening cocktail, a Manhattan for me, and Sauvignon Blanc for Joanie. The colour of the berry skins was turning from yellow to green and softening as sugar accumulated. We had reduced the heavy canopy of leaves to accelerate the final ripening.

"I distrust Deo's bouts of euphoria," Joanie replied.

"I find them hard to resist," I disagreed, taking a belt of my Manhattan.

"The crash will come," Joanie warned. "He vibrates at too high a frequency."

"I get infected by the high temperature of his existence," I said.

"It's a toxic contagion of vitality, Joanie replied.

A pall joined us under the portico.

I wasn't prepared to let go. "What do you think he meant by the 'underbellies of the world?" I asked, prying Joanie away from her article in the New Yorker.

"Tucked away people?" Joanie replied. "Like the forest tribes of New Guinea?"

"Or maybe the ghettos and slums of the world," I added.

A silence settled as the sun mottled the front orchard in streaks of light.

"Isn't the world filled with decent people who are simply trying to get through the day? Joanie pondered aloud.

"Maybe," I said. "but I don't think they are the illuminati Deo is referring to?"

I hadn't quite finished.

"Once we find these authentic people," I asked, "what are we supposed to do with their bon mots of wisdom?"

"Lock them in a vault," Joanie joked in a determined attempt to return to her article. "And throw away the keys until the world regains its senses."

"I would opt for acknowledgement," I replied to counter the seeping skepticism of our conversation. "Something like 'yabo sawuybona."

Joanie looked up wide-eyed as a fox in headlights.

"Swahili for 'I see your soul'," I explained.

A few days later I found the courage to raise the possibility again with Joanie. Something I had begun to think of as an 'A –Quest' - a search for everyday wisdom. I didn't want her blessing so much as an 'imprimatur of sanity' for the undertaking that was in my head. I suggested a walk at Sandbanks. The fact that we had trails much closer to home must have set off alarm bells. She probably expected an awkward conversation, or maybe a confrontation. I think part of her wanted to be included in the swashbuckling odyssey Deo has mapped out for me. A small part of her was trying to believe.

"You have the elements," she began. "Saitarg has a singular power to root out enlightenment, you have a mission to preserve wisdom, and a cape to protect you."

"Maybe we could undertake a dry run," I said capitalizing on her encouragement. "And test our approach on someone nearby."

"Someone we have never met?" she queried with a flourish. "A stranger who holds the promise of 'sagacity'?"

I let the idea settle, mulling over the possibility of an individual nearby, perhaps a neighbour in North Marysburgh, who might be a test for our hypothetical quest. We knew almost all of our immediate community on County Road 8, between Picton and Prinyer's Cove. It was Joanie, the skeptic and Deo-basher, who made the breakthrough. We were having dinner in the library when the first chill of the autumn season had surrendered to an applewood blaze in the fireplace.

"What about the new resident in the Saxon House," Joanie suggested as we sat down for poached salmon at the table behind the sofa.

"Does he really exist?" I said, "We just suppose that someone like him is the cause for Roger's recent behaviour."

"That makes him the perfect candidate for our test journey," Joanie concluded, clinking my recharged wine glass.

Although she may have been indulging my imaginary quest, I had the impression that Joanie wanted to be included in a clandestine trip to the Saxon House.

Discovering ourselves – one question at a time

Gravitassing is a Latin word derived from 'gravitas' which emeans substance or depth of personality. Turned into a verb, 'to gravitas' means to access inner reserves of wisdom, insight, and savoir faire. To gravitas is to use our life experiences to the best we can.
'Gravitassing' then becomes the practice of discovering and expressing the meaning of our experiences. In short it is our take on what we have learned along the way.
Gravitassing embodies the search for authenticity, the need to connect with real people in real time, and to escape the insulating effects of our social media gadgets.

The new mantra becomes 'Have you gravitassed today?'
A Gravitarg is the highest rank, the others being a Sage and a Savant, in the Order of Gravitatis which is a council of wise people who help Count Saitarg collect and preserve deposits of individual wisdoms, insights and savoir faire.
Count Saitarg and his Gravitargs, along with Saitarg's Supersleuth Dog, Rogerio, live deep beneath the earth's crust in a realm devoted to discovering, preserving, and sharing reserves of gravitas.
Saitarg, or Count Saitarg as his correct title, is the contemporary incarnation of The Wise Spirit, a Wayfinder who is re-imagined from time to time. His mission is to empower the human software to utilize individual reserves of gravitas.
The benediction of 'Saitarg' is composed of two equal parts. 'Sait' a French word meaning 'he knows', and 'arg' which connotes an otherworldly existence. The goal of Saitargism is to realize potential, or as Confucius would say 'happy thinking'.
Saitarg's First Law is "an individual's achieved wisdom is the gateway to fulfillment." Every human has the responsibility to access, act on, and share their inner reserves of wisdom and experience. As the Grand Gravitarg, Saitarg is the leader of the Gravitargs, people of special illumination.

The Questions

The template or methodology for the questions is straight forward and divided into three categories
Question that relate essential to how you have lived your life and your behaviours (personal); questions that speak more to larger philosophical views about how the world works (profound), and finally more open-ended, quirky questions that are open to many interpretations (singular)

Personal (vanitas) - how have you lived your life?

What do you really care about?
What do you use for an in-house aphrodisiac?
What is your technique for reading faces?
Name one universal rule of friendship?
We all fall into categories. What category are you in?
What do you think about someone who doesn't like animals?
Describe your first apparition.
What are you going to do about growing old?
How can we give our self-esteem a boost?
If you wanted to disappear, where would you go?
Give an example of how you think outside the box.
What is your inner imperative?
How do I get to live your life?
What have you not got from your life?

Give an example of a mixed blessing in life.
Describe an out of body experience you have had.
How do you take a vacation from yourself?
What makes someone really sexy?
How can you tell your partner is trying to break up with you?
What is your standard for a reckless life?
What ranks after good sex for a happy marriage?
How can you tell love is in the air?
What gets you blessed out?
What place does music take you to?
What makes your heart stand still?
What happens when love goes wrong?
Give an example of a hidden gem.
What is a good way not to make an impact?
Why does your high school sweetheart cause you angst?
What recipe for a successful home life do you want to share?
If you knew the truth, how would you reveal it?
What first step are you proudest of?
We all hope there will be one more time. One more time for what?
They say everyone should have a cause. What is your cause?
What is the best cure for love?
If you wanted to steal a heart away, what would you do?
Where is the worst place you have gone on a date?
What is your path to redemption?
What is your technique for keeping cool?
When was your last rapture?
How do you liberate your ego?
Name one secret you do not want to discover before you die?
Tell me one thing you never do?
If there were a recipe for a goo life, what ingredient would you like to contribute?
If you were overcome with exuberance, what would you do?
When do you push the off button on your hyperactive mind?
What is your addiction?
What are you not free to have?
What are you missing on any given day?
Tell your life story in six words.
Give an example of your best multitasking.
On what grounds can you claim moral superiority?

If you were going to launch a new prohibition, what would you outlaw?
If you were Zen, what would you be?
What is your road map to bliss?
How would you like to rewire your brain?
What is your secret adorable being?
What is the best way to deal with your baggage?
What is the strongest message you received from your parents?
Why does passion reverse its course more swiftly than other emotions?
What is the strongest message your received from your parents?
If you were to ask for divine intervention, what would it be for?
What makes your spirit soar?
How can you embrace your inner divinity?
How do you hold steady in a chaotic world?
When you hear that love is in the air, what do you do?
What happens when you don't listen to that inner voice?
With the benefit of hindsight, name one thing you would do differently.
What should we blame our mothers for?
What do you want out of life?
When would you like to spank your partner?
What is a view to die for?
What is the best way to stay in love?
How do you restore your equilibrium?
When are you in your element?
What is your proud madness?
What gets you out of bed in the morning?
How would you like to rearrange your rigidities?
What are you fatally attracted to?
What is your own legend?
What do you want to rebel against?
What would you like royalty rights for?
When you say you want to live in the moment, what moment is that?
What is the best way to look your fate in the eye?
What happened to your teddy bear?
What is the worst comment a teacher made about you on your report card?
What makes your soul tremble?
When do you feel the most grounded?
What makes you feel helpless?
What are the dangers of a reckless heart?

What tyranny would you most like to be free of?
What is the best way to mend a broken heart?
Why does the euphoria of first love ruin all the others?
Name one non-sexual way to cheat on your partner.
What are the pitfalls of being too happy?
Give an example of the kooky, adventuresome ways of women.
When should we say it out loud?
What are the advantages of self-absorption?
Why can only unrealized love be romantic?
What is the essence of flirtation?
Why is love so hard to define?
How would you describe the scent of your partner?
If you were assigned a life coach with a mandate to change you, what would you get the coach to do?
How do you shake things up?
Name one powerful indicator of happiness?
What is the most generous thing you have ever done?
What is the best way to make someone fall in love with you?
What book have you lied about reading?
Give an example of how God is in the details.
What makes your spirit soar?
Name one universal rule of a successful marriage?
What is the best way to deal with confusion?
What is the best way to outfox fate?
What is the best way to reconnect to your inner creative child?
Name one secret you should always keep from your partner.
When does flirtation become seduction?
Why are men so inept at reading non-verbal clues from women?
Why does charm always trump good looks?
What is the worst thing you have been caught doing?
What is the worst thing you have never caught doing?
What can you tell from that first kiss?
What is your favourite thing to do when you joints don't ache?
Give an example of receiving something you needed but did not want.
What is the most important life lesson you have learned so far?
What would you like to morph yourself into?
How can we adjust our default position so that we are not the center of the universe?
How can we escape our inner wounded child?

What kitchen appliance do you find the most ridiculous?
Now that it is over what is the best thing you can say about your 'ex'?
What triggers an epiphany in you?
What is the first requisite of happiness?
How do you know you are about to have an epiphany?
If your pet could talk what would she say about your private life?
Define great looking?
How do you measure someone's humanity?
How do you know you have come into contact with a beautiful mind?
What is the motherlode for you?
Why is it better to be too loved than not loved enough?
If you dream big, what do you dream about?
What is the best surprise you have found in a shoebox?
What pack do you run with?
What is happiness?
What do you wish you understood about your mother?
Where are going to store your soul?
Why all the train wrecks around you?
How do you know you are happy?
What is the heaviest component of your life?
Why is it better to be madly in love than madly loved?
How have you wimped out?
What is your standard for wimpishness?
Who would you most like to hug?
Give an example of how the unlived lives of our parents influence their children.
When is the last time you experienced the Freudian phrase 'oceanic rapture'?
What do you want to deny?
What is your most life-affirming experience in the last year?
What takes your breath away?
At what point do you surrender?
What happens when pursuit ends, and possession begins?
How can you be saved from yourself?
How can we be alone without being lonely?
What makes you unhappy?
What is your favourite word?
When they say you have to walk the talk, what talk?
What is the height of nonsense?

How do you live your best life?
Name one universal rule of getting a good night's sleep.
How do I get to your dark side?
What is the best way to get excited about your life?
Why should we never tell the truth to our mothers?
If you had to be flawed, what flaw would you like to be saddled with?
What is your big idea?
What is it that you are seeking?
What is your hidden talent?
How can we acquire charm?
If you wanted a romantic getaway, what would you do?
If you wanted to be suffused with something, what would you like to be suffused with?
What can you tell from that first kiss?
What is the last thing you will abandon on your path to pure detachment?
What is your most valuable instrument of peace?
Name one good thing about jealousy?
Who is the unknown presence at your side?
What is the best way to discover who you are?
What is your ego's job?
What is the best way to quiet the mind?
What was your last delirious experience?
What have you done to transform your consciousness?
When do you need a leap of faith?
What is the most redeeming aspect of parenting?
Relationships are ripe with irrational behaviour. Name one.
Why should we read fiction?
What makes some women so exciting?
What is the greatest pleasure in life?
What truth about yourself would you like other people to know?
Why is it better to have sexual fantasies than experience the reality?
What makes us susceptible to charm?
What do you do when you fall apart?
What makes some men so boring?
Where can we find the best roadmap for the soul?
What is your interior fiction?
How should dreams begin?
What ends would you like to tie up?
What makes you feel the most uncomfortable?

What is the source of your happiness?
What are you trying to perfect?
What is the essence of good taste?
What makes a great kitchen?
Why would you want to live forever?
What are benefits of having suffered from a psychological depression?
How do you come to terms with your transgressions?
How would you characterize the happiness gap between men and women?
How can we get out of our own way?
What makes you feel the person you are the most?
Why do we need agitation in our lives?
Why is it better to be self-confident that grounded?
What is it about self confidence that is so essential?
What have been the right words at the right time for you?
What are the advantages of being a late bloomer?
What is the best way to get out of a funk?
What is the best way to out the truth?
What is the secret of growing old with élan?
What made you realize you had become yourself?
What is your standard for too much sex?
Why do women find vulnerability in men so attractive?
How are fashionistas the antennae of our times?
Knowing what you know about university life, what advice you would give a first-year entrant?
What are you going to do about your carbon footprint?
Name one thing you are going to do soon because you have not done it yet.
If you were a dream therapist, what would you make of your dreams?
What is the best way to figure out what is on someone's mind?
What is that we like about living in the shadows?
Life is about compromise. How have you compromised?
What is your unknown compulsion?
Who gives you the fever?
If you really want something to happen, how can you make it happen?
How can we be everything we want to be?
How do you know you have reached middle age?
If you follow your heart, where will it lead you?
Which of your strengths can lead to problems?

Tell me the great idea you had but didn't do anything about?
What do you really crave?
What makes for an extraordinary muse?
How do you know you are having an "aha" moment?
What pleasures have you taken that you ought not to have?
When is self-absorption healthy?
Give an example of how feelings can lead you astray.
What nightclub act would you like to star in?
How do you know you have left your youth behind?
Where do you draw the line in what you will share?
How do the gods punish you?
Why do we desire what we do not have?
What is your story?
When do we say one thing and mean another?
When do we most need endurance?
Tell me one simple truth.
What are you hunting?
What small thing gives you a feeling of being well off?
What would you sell your soul for?
What one compliment would you like to receive?
What is the secret to achieving serenity?
What is the best cure for the fear of death?
What is the ceaseless labour of your life all about?
What do you whisper about?
When is it okay to seek revenge?
What excuse do you use to hang out with your friends?
Who is that behind you?
What make a great lover?
How do you choose what to think about?
How do you explain your sex appeal?
What is the key to understanding how you think?
What doesn't have enough magic for you?
What is the most important piece of advice you would give to a man about to be married?
Give an example of your everyday crazy.
Why is there only chaos and blur in our private mind?
What is your first rule of etiquette?
What lands you in a 'cul de sac'?
How do you decipher what God is trying to tell you?

When do you need a muse?
Where did you go wrong?
How do you know turbulence is coming?
What is the best way to grow up fast?
Why is the desire to do something we know we will regret, sometimes overwhelming?
How can you recognize how happy you are?
When do your demons slip their leash?
What keeps you sane?
When do you switch off your moral code?
How does the supernatural work for you?
When does your pleasure become your pain?
What feelings do you love the most?
When do you lose faith in yourself?
How are you the captain of your soul?
Why are so under-realized?
What is your life's work?
How do you measure the sum of your life?
How have you brought joy to others?
How do you plan to outsmart old?
Sacrifice is derived from the Latin 'to make sacred'. What has made you sacred?
What's it like to live alone inside your head?
How do we inspire ourselves to greatness?
How can you exceed your own expectations?
How are we ruled by our hormones?
What tools have allowed you to survive this cutthroat world?
What scientific question would you most like to have answered?
How do you know if there is greatness in you?
Why is it better to have charm than charisma?
Who would you like to have a conversation of a lifetime with?
What does your sibling really think about you?
How will you measure your life?
How do you take the scary out of life?
How do you stay clear of the rocks and shoals?
Where do you go in search of the fading light?
How are all your riches interior riches?
What is your favourite recipe for unhappiness?
How can you make your ideal a reality?

When they say ‘follow the fear’, why fear are you following?
If it is never too late to be what you might have been, what might you have been?
If provenance is all, what is your provenance?
If you wanted to show the world your fire, what would you light?
If you were in charge of the world for one day, what would you change?
What takes you down the rabbit hole?
If we become what we think, what are you thinking?
What is the surest way to beguile you?
What makes you absurdly happy?
Where do you go to find beautiful undiscovered things?
What takes you to a place where nothing else matters?
Where do you go to practice the lost art of solitude?
Who is your muse?
How are you going to find your greatness?
What have you learned about the best way to say good-bye?
What is the second thing you do every morning?
What type of idea are you?
‘Wa’ time is a Japanese expression meaning peacefulness of spirit. When is your ‘wa’ time?
How can you get your swagger back?
What is the one question you want to ask?
Why does your life not look like anything you had imagined?
What things have you done that you would like to undo?
How are you a parody of what you thought you would be?
If you had rewind in your life, how would you use it?
What is one thing you wish you knew at twenty-one?
How can you take control of the narrative?
How do you know you are loved?
If you were the supreme lawmaker, what would you ban?
How do you know you have found your perfect place?
How did you get to be who you are today?
What increases your sense of reverence?
What best represents the person you once aspired to be?
How can you avoid not ending up a parody of what you thought you were?
In what way are you more beautiful than you think?
In what way are you wiser than you think?
In what way are you more evil than you think?

When do you release your inner quirkiness?
When do you fly your freak flag?
If we come into this world with sealed orders, what are your orders?
How do you reinvent yourself?
What shocks and appalls you?
How are you different from the way others perceive you?

How do you decide what to think about?
If you had your own country, what is the first law you would enact?
How do you work mindful meditation into your everyday life?
What are you going to do about your decline?
How can you gain a new soul?
What do you talk about when you talk about love?
Deep down we all hug something. The forest hugs its silence. The sea hugs the spilled cries of gulls. What do you hug deep down?
Tell me one secret to a good life.
How can you gain a new soul?
What do you talk about when you talk about love?
Finish the sentence, "whoever falls in love with me is in trouble because............"
They say it is what you hide that makes you interesting. What are you hiding?
We are measured in the difference we make in other people's lives. What difference have you made?
The whole point of being an artist is to learn about you. What have you learned about yourself?
What is the best advice you ever received?
They say we tell stories to keep our raft afloat. What story to you tell?
The ability to endure through change is the miracle of selfhood. What changes have you endured?
Taking ourselves apart and rebuilding is human nature. How have you taken yourself apart?
When you stop long enough to cry, what do you cry about?
Tell me something that shows you have grown up enough to know the truth about yourself.
What does 'belonging to a community' mean to you?
If 'need' is a wild animal, what wild animal need do you harbor?
They say that only when things fall apart, can you see what they are made of? When do things fall apart for you?

How do you escape the prison-house of your own self?
How do you explain your own particularity?
If you have lost the faith, how can you get it back?
If you wanted to unlock the secrets to eternal life, what would you do?

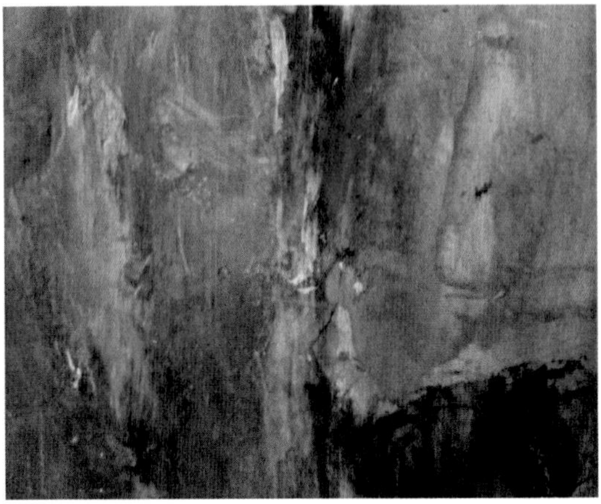

Profound (gravitas) - let me think about that

Why is there always conflict in the human heart?
Why should we feel more and think less?
What is the hallmark of a good person?
What makes us care?
When does it all begin?
Where is the best place to start?
Why do we never say it all?
Name one universal rule of attractions?
What do any of us know about each other?
Why is it that the more we know, the more we suffer?
What is the best way to get our confidence back?
What is the point of all the struggle?
How are we hard wired to the supernatural?
What are the advantages of being small and staying small?
Why is there so much fog around the moral high ground?
What is the downside of wealth?
How do you figure out the worth of something?
Name one common denominator that predicts longevity?
What can we learn from rejection?
Why do we so often look but not see?
What is it about truthfulness that is scary
Why should we tolerate ambiguity?
Why are humans so fragile?
Why does the world need more of the poetic sensibility?
What is the power of the weak?
Why do we have to prove we are the best?
How can we live out our loneliness?
How does weakness bring us together?
What is the most authentic form of belonging?
Name one universal benefit of using our imagination.
How do you know an era has come to an end?
How can you become who you are meant to be?
What is the essence of atonement?
When should we give in?
Where do we always find the answer?
Name one thing we should feel entitled to.
What is the well spring of addictions?
Give an example of a stubbornly persistent illusion.
What is the wisdom of uncertainty?

Why is danger sometimes so alluring?
What's wrong with 'normal'?
What is it about spiritual consolation that is so satisfying?
How are the two states of birth and death the same?
What is the essence of integrity?
What is not what it seems?
How can you avoid truth falling on deaf ears?
Why should we be skeptical of those who have found the truth?
Why is it good to have footpaths and not roads?
Why do women live longer than men?
Why do we sometimes crave chaos?
Why is the first cut the deepest?
When does 'think' end and 'know begin'?
Name one tenet of the art of forgiveness?
In what way is it never too late to be the person you might have been?
How can you prepare someone to handle the truth?
Why do sinners flourish?
What is it that we need to understand about surrender?
Why do we need stories?
What is the supreme happiness?
How would you characterize the difference between how men and women talk?
What is the essence of seduction?
Give an example of how truth is stranger than fiction.
Name one universal rule of persuasion.
Summarize the game of life
Why do we go to the sea?
Why don't we act on the things we have learned in life?
When should we start thinking about the beginning?
What is so appealing about vulnerability?
What can we learn from the weak and vulnerable?
Why does the journey have no end?
What excites the mind and the heart in equal measure?
Why are we so interested in the interior lives of strangers?
They say that the greatest love is never shown. What love have you never shown?
If you break down the truth into its constituent parts, what do you get?
What is the only hope?
Why do we long for moments of beginnings when the course is set?

What is wrong with a democracy?
How are emotions the bedrock of our existence?
Pleasure in nature's way of saying what?
How can we be rescued from our own fate?
When is it better to be a follower than a leader?
Why is love so hard to define?
In what way does hardship beget enlightenment?
What is the function of dysfunction?
What is the most exciting part of collapse?
What is the best way to classify people?
What if everything in the universe is aware of everything else?
How is the possession of memory possession of the soul?
How does each of us become a new person as we describe the past?
What are the limits of words?
What is the link between doing good and living longer?
What did Shakespeare mean when he said "it is not in the stars but in us"?
How can the meek get empowered?
How can we unlock the secrets of time?
What are the limitations of experience?
Why is life worth living?
What is the best way to handle bad news?
How is wit a treacherous talent?
When can doubt be as sustaining an emotion as certainty?
They say that what brings out together is stronger than what pulls out apart. What pulls us apart?
How is the mind an excellent servant but a terrible master?
What is the most important freedom?
To forgive or to revenge - how do you decide?
At the end of the day why do women always wear the pants?
Why is it so easy to fall in love?
What is the best way to fight apathy?
How do you know you are dealing with an intellectual?
Why is happiness so brief?
Why is character better kept than recovered?
How is love a kind of wound?
When do words get in the way?
What food preparation job do you most dread?
In what way is love the great adventure hiding in the nape of the lion?

In what way does the Truth set us free?
Where does great art come from?
How can we reconnect to our roots?
What are drugs a mask for?
How is addiction a choice?
In what way does the universe have no edges?
Why is everyone powerfully attracted to fame?
Why are we a failed species?
What journeys change mankind forever?
If beauty is in the passing, how can we hold on?
Why do things start to go wrong when individuals get together in groups?
Why is it that as people age they become more like themselves?
What did Freud mean when he said 'there are no accidents in life'?
In what way is reality arbitrary?
Why does love matter?
What is the secret to accomplishing great things in our world?
What is the well spring of envy?
Name one universal rule of achieving balance in your life?
How can pain bring us closer to the truth?
In what way is the moment the perfect teacher?
Why is the unflawed life not worth living?
What is it that distinguished the human species from all others?
Name one issue that all species fight about?
What does death require of us?
What is the downside of happiness?
What distinguishes chaos from control?
How can we expose the truth?
How can we negotiate the no-man's land between good and evil?
How can we transcend our ego-based consciousness?
What does not go away?
What cannot be taught?
What is the essence of a good prayer?
What is the basic difference between men and women?
When can ugly be beautiful?
Why should we let things go a bit wild?
Why is it more important to have memories than a future?
What is the truth behind all lies?
What are the costs of popularity?
Name one universal rule of good manners.

When is fear an appropriate response?
Why does a hungry life lead to a longer life?
Give an example of what people will believe to get them through the day?
What is the best way to deal with moral break down?
What questions are best left unanswered?
Why is vice so much more interesting than virtue?
What is forever?
In what way are we what we think?
Why are some people so restless to seek extraordinary experiences?
Give one example of life's absurdities?
What is so galling about pretention?
Why do women not hold secrets from each other?
Why should we make a friend of fear?
What is the best way to express love?
When do ordinary people do extraordinary things?
What can fragility teach us?
What is the world's last great hope?
Why is age a work of art?
What is the key to seeing beauty?
What is the best way to get noticed?
How can we differentiate ourselves?
What is the best way to tell a story?
Why does too much choice make us unhappy?
Why the beauty of haphazardness?
Name one universal rule of cleanliness?
What journeys cannot be put into words?
What would we do without unhappiness?
When does desire end and duty begin?
Why are couples the most mysterious creation?
Name one good way to live on nature's income rather than nature's capital.
What is the best way to judge someone's intelligence?
Why is rebellion so enjoyable?
Why should we believe in those who are looking for the truth rather than those who have found it?
What is long lived in shadow and short lived in sunlight?
What is the best way to measure a person's resilience?
How do you know when to say good-bye?
Name one universal truth about infidelity.

What makes a city livable?
How is a room a metaphor for our state of being?
What are the advantages of diversity over uniformity?
What is the difference between fashion and style?
Why is truth telling easier from a distance?
Why does flirtation never end?
What is the best measure of a society's well-being?
What is forever?
What is the surest indicator of intelligence?
Why do we need boundaries?
What is the ultimate act of rebellion?
How can we account for the gift of silence?
Why is it that everything we seem to be totally certain about turns out to be wrong?
How do you decide what has meaning and what does not?
What is the most precious of all freedoms?
What is the secret to delaying gratification?
What is the best way to measure strength of character?
How do you teach self–control?
How can we outsmart our desires?
What is the best way to recognize awesome?
When should we talk to strangers?
How are artists the antennae of the human race?
How can we increase our capacity for happiness?
Why is attachment such a difficult thing to undo?
What is the best way to screw our courage to the sticking place?
How is romantic love a drug?
Why do we yearn for a re-enchantment with the natural world?
In what way is the rational mind a faithful servant?
Why is it that only what exists in the imagination is imperishable?
How can you find out about your destiny?
What is it about a woman's touch?
What if everything in the world is aware of everything else?
In what way is possession of memory possession of the soul?
How do each of us become a new person as we remember the past?
How are people changed by how we classify them?
Why is self –delusion so inescapable?
How is hell the truth learned too late?
In what way is the intuitive mind a sacred gift?

Why can't the authorities stand the truth?
Why is it that everything we know, we know because of love?
How can we see with our minds instead of just with our eyes?
What is so menacing about orthodoxy?
When should we learn to be unhappy?
How can we discover the truth?
Why should status be accorded to the person of wisdom instead of the rich?
How is the smallest grain of sand a mirror of the universe?
Why should we embrace solitude?
In what way is the lowering of expectations the beginning of wisdom?
Why does altruism exist in the natural world?
How can forgiveness set you free?
Why do we take comfort in rituals?
How do you explain the healing power of the human imagination?
How do you know the order of things?
Why is forgiveness such a powerful weapon?
What do you understand of the essential connectedness of all humanity?
When does a man become most human?
Why do we call it love?
How can we know Destiny's intentions?
How do landscape and place make people more knowable?
Why are we lured into the unknown?
Why is it that the more we find out, the more the mystery deepens?
Why should we hang onto our illusions?
How do you know what questions to ask?
What shapes attitude?
Why is it that most writers are only interested in themselves?
What do we possess with absolute certainty?
Why are the best things in life not things?
Why do people have a need for drama in their lives?
Why do we try to make our life into a fairy tale?
When do reality and fantasy merge?
What is the best way to find love?
Why is memory deliberately distorting?
What is the best way to get licensed as an adult?
Why does revenge rarely live up to expectations?
Why do we lack willpower?
How do we become who we are?

If life is flux, how does the self adapt?
How is art a lie that helps us see the truth?
How do we get to the authentic self?
What do you wish you understood about the workings of the universe?
When is it important to sound convincing without expertise?
What evolutionary purpose does nostalgia serve?
If life is a wager, what form does the bet take?
When they say that time finds out, finds out what?
When do our best supported decisions seem wobbly?
How do you know life is not everything it is cracked up to be?
If something has to collapse before something is born, what would you like to collapse?
Why the eternal hopefulness of the human heart?
Why is it the longer we live, the less we understand?
How can you make the darkness visible?
How is life nothing but suffering?
Why will man not give up his suffering?
How can we live conventional lives with unconventional perspectives?
In what way is silence the warrior's art?
How can we show kindness and compassion when we don't feel it?
How is the world far more interesting than our thoughts about it?
What is the importance of ceremony?
What is the difference between feeling happy and acting happy?
What is it that we are all truly seeking?
Why is a sense of superiority an illusion?
What is it about love that cannot be understood?
Why do our greatest strengths and profound frailties remain hidden?
Why does perseverance count more than ideas?
How can you go with joy among the sorrows of the world?
How is life theatre?
How can we rethink humankind's bonds to nature?
How are we formed by what we desire?
In what way are we hard wired for pleasure?
In what way are humans, like all mammals, hard wired in function in groups?
What we should be forbidden from laughing at.
When you look into the void, what do you see?
Why do people see more than they think proper to say?
Why does the world exist?

How is wisdom the epic side of truth?
In what way is the philosopher nature's pilot?
Why are humans hard wired for story telling?
How are we changed by the stories we tell?
When is fiction as much a reality as reality?
Why the enduring appeal of the apocalypse?
Why does man need escape as much as he needs food and sleep?
Why is very little needed to make a happy life?
How does the truth reveal itself slowly?
When desire comes in the door, why does judgment jump out the window?
Why are the falsest judgments the most indispensable to us?
In what way is chaos the way of nature, and order the dream of man?
Why do we need to challenge the wisdom of old men?
What things gain from disorder?
How can we teach ourselves the meaning of life?
How can we get life to squeeze the best out of us?
How should a person be?
When should we look into the abyss?
How can we get to live in a state of grace?
What does your existence mean?
How is gratitude the beginning of compassion?
Why is humility such a powerful force?
Why do the deepest feelings always present in silence?
Why the urge to return to origins?
What is the key to survival?
Why do we sometimes have to lie to find the truth?
What is it about editing that is so compulsive?
Why are the wicked sometimes triumphant?
What is the least attractive addiction of the human species?
How do you know a good soul?
Why is losing good?
Why is every human creature a mystery to each other?
Why do things from the heart not need an explanation?
Why the human longing for transcendence?
How is every love the same love?
How can we improve on truth?
Why are all great quests folly?
When should we live out loud?

Why is almost all love hopeless?
Why does the present moment elude us completely?
Why does nature always win?
Why is everything the way it is?
Why must we reconcile with the past?
What is the one question that never goes away?
Why is the heart a lonely hunter?
What endures?
How do we earn our wisdom?
What do they mean when they say 'wherever you go, there you are'?
Why does every great thing begin with a question?
Why does anything exist?
Give an example of how every great thing begins with a question?
How do you account for life's periodic renewals?
How can old age become a second childhood?
What is the virtue of ignorance?
Why do we feel the pain of loss more than the pleasure of gain?
What does it mean for something to be?
What if everything we know is a dream?
How do you find peace in chaos?
When they say the truth is implausible, what do they mean?
How do you explain the tenacity of life?
How are humans the agency of their own demise?
Why is it better to perch and not settle in?
If you cannot live alone, you were born a slave. Comment.
Each one of us has the responsibility to turn negative experiences into positive experiences. How do you do it?
Why is knowledge more important than beliefs, opinions or suspicions?
Why do the dead have such a grip on the living?
How do intellectual passions subdue sensuality?
How is life the sum of all your choices?
How is food the best weapon in the world for peace?
Why is it the fate of every successful species to wipe itself out?

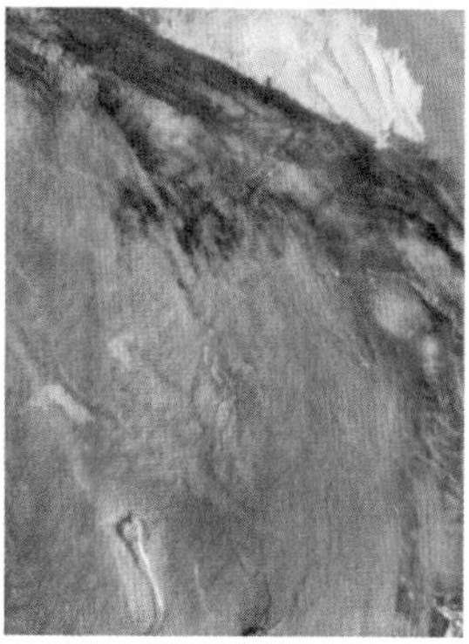

Singular (levitas) - no one has ever asked me that

Where is Roger?
What is your theory why humans started to walk upright instead of on all fours?
How can we get our mojo back?
Name one good thing about declining levels of testosterone?
When do nerds go wild?
How does a woman know for sure?
What is the first question your in-laws asked you when they found out?
Why should we should avoid the term 'relationship'?
Why is it if we are not living beyond our means, we are not living at all?
Give an example of how a guy can be a lot of work?
What if we are living in a computer simulation?
If you are not a talker or thinker, what are you?

When is the last chance to be the person you want to be?
Why do we love jazz more as we grow older?
Why are some people so affected by the phases of the moon?
What would Roger do?
What else does she want?
Why do women not make sense?
What question do you wish you never asked?
Give an example of saying very little and being profound.
If you were asked to dance to the music of time, what would you do?
When should we capitulate to the unknown?
What is the essence of a great miracle?
Who would you be without your briefcase?
What is the essence of post-coital?
Why are men so ridiculous?
What happens on your planet?
Name one reason to marry a Prairie partner?
Give an example of the power of suggestion
Say what ain't so?
Make up a Hippocratic Oath for relationships?
Name one good thing about suffering.
When should we go into a huddle?
How do you decide which bridge to cross?
How do you decide which bridge to burn?
How do you decide which bridge is too far?
How can the hurricane within you be released?
What are the attributes of a great cuddle?
Why do men still think they rule the world?
Name one good thing about bewilderment?
What would you like your personal firewall to protect you against?
Give an example of a great place that is not found on any map.
Why do some people try so hard to be loved?
Why do women love disclosure?
Why is sloth so appealing?
Name one good thing about guilt.
What is the essence of an intoxicating perfume?
How is love like slowly losing your mind?
How would you like to rearrange your rigidities?
What do you think of a guy who has fifty pair of shoes?
What do you think of a guy who wears a codpiece?

When is it time to climb on the ice-floes?
When should men go wild?
How can we figure it all out?
When are there happy endings?
Give an example of the ‘panky’ in ‘hanky panky’.
If you were going to heckle someone, what would you say?
What do you have left?
Why do we love to binge from time to time?
Name one thing the nose knows.
Under what circumstances would you wear your partner’s underwear?
What is the secret to getting back on the dance card?
Who most needs bragging rights?
Why can we never know someone else’s truth?
How do you know someone is lonely?
When is it good to exercise shopping therapy?
What are the advantages of unsupervised introspection?
What would you do if, like a dog, you always had a wet nose?
When does a guy not think of sex?
Why do men go bald?
What is the best way to make your pet jealous?
What makes a nerd so sexy?
What is the difference between a hunk and a nerd?
Why is the perfect affair never perfect?
When is unrequited love enough?
Why is anything worth knowing not known through the brain?
Why is narcissism so attractive?
When should we pull the trap door?
How do you know if you are dealing with a devil?
What happens to humans if they can have all the food and sex they want?
If you had to practice cannibalism what condiments would you insist on?
How does the story end?
Why is the brain an overrated organ?
What is the best way to test your pet’s IQ?
Why do we have to suffer to look beautiful’?
What is the best way to move from one god to another?
What is best not realized?
How do you know your dinner party is really cooking?
Why do orchestra conductors live so long?
Name one law of physics you would like to change.

Why would you rather be part of the great unwashed than the over perfumed?
What makes a born liar?
How do you know you are dealing with an angel?
How are rodents beautiful?
Why do artists lead the way?
What do they mean when they talk about 'the orgiastic future'?
What is the best part of the story?
What can you tell about someone who wears tight pants?
When should sensible replace passion?
What if we only exist as a character in a story?
Why do musicians always attract the most passionate partners?
What is it that gothic is trying to do?
What does 'frisson' bring to our lives?
When do you feel only a few rogue cells away from the end?
What does a woman really mean when she says "I love your outfit"?
In what area do you consider yourself a maven?
Why do most women remember their first shoe purchase more than their first kiss?
If you were a God in a new planet, what is the first thing you would do?
Why will Italian take you a long way?
When someone says 'that colour looks great on you', what do they really mean?
How are bartending skills a good proxy for what it takes to get through life?
Why the thrill of the dancing zombie?
What is the best way to get your shirt untucked?
Why are the men depicted in ads so goofy, dumb and inert?
Why do some people enjoy getting naked so much?
What is the first sign that the party is over?
What is a good incentive to get the kids to leave home?
How can we distill life and style into one?
Complete the sentence "shoes are to women as ----- is to men".
What is the best way to travel far and fast?
Name one universal characteristic of a martini drinker?
How do you know you are being seduced?
Name one great thing about being bald.
How can you stop what's coming?
When should we liberate the angels in marble?

How do you know for sure?
What should we not blow out?
What happens when we practice too much civility?
When do Gods behave badly?
Why do men and women have such different standards of cleanliness?
Why is lighting so important?
Name one speed bump on the road to enlightenment.
When does your hair tell the story?
When they say that your hair tells the story, what story?
How can we coax enchantment from the most prosaic of settings?
How can we reintroduce charm into the vale of mud and tears known as modern life?
When is it better to have charm and wit than talent and intelligence?
Why are divas so much fun?
Why do humans deteriorate faster than their pets?
How do you know you are ready to party?
Why do some people lose their mojo?
What is the best way to smell a rat?
Why do men honk more than women?
What does it take to be a cerebral stud?
Give an example of a sublime lunacy?
When is a hug more than hug?
What are the attributes of a great kiss?
What is it about being on the cusp that is so great?
When is a hug better than a kiss?
Give an example of a desperate measure.
Give an example of flying under false colours.
Why are we all fools when it comes to love?
When is it okay to be a rotter?
When is speaking with an accent an advantage?
What are the disadvantages of a hugely creative personality?
Give an example of an abuse of time?
Why do only the paranoid survive?
What will happen next?
What would you do?
What is it about the maverick that is so annoying?
What would you do if your lover called you 'babycakes'?
What should inspiration be coupled with to produce genius?
Give an example of body language that accompanies deception.

What do you do when the goofy talk begins?
Why does it never end?
How would you describe today's middle-aged man?
Where do you want your fermentation to start?
How can we get the good times rolling?
What is that we love about nuns?
When should we wear our tightest pants?
Show me some moves of the previously unknown dance craze the ' hokipoki'.
If you could have the power of a superhero, what power would you choose?
Show me your best dance move.
How does the new sexy differ from the old sexy?
Why do owners become increasingly like their pets?
What is the 'naked singularity' of your life?
What lasts?
How can you make it happen?
How is life like a huge grapefruit?
Show me your best dirty dancing?
How can you earn the right to be a diva?
Name one thing we can do in old age that we couldn't young.
What is the best way to show mileage on our face?
Name one rule of anger management.
What works for you?
What's good about self-absorption?
Why should we praise 'slow'?
What if we are only playthings in a universe of aimless fate?
What is it about the concept of 'shoehorning' that is so attractive?
Who should be in charge?
When Milton talks of 'the amorous delay of life in Eden", what he is getting at?
What is the difference between a good silence and a bad silence?
How can you tell your dog is smarter than mine?
How can we keep old at bay?
How can we short-circuit old?
Why do women always wear black?
What can not be orchestrated?
Why is it that only our ears keeps growing as we age?
How did you do it?

What is good about fat?
What is the most important attribute of a great spy?
When does the hunt end?
Show me your best twaddle.
Why should we toast the misfits and crazies of our world?
The female tarantula eats their male suitor after copulation. What lessons there?
What is the best way to deal with love sickness?
What does it take?
Why do women love intensity in a man?
Why are we drawn to magnificent bastards?
What is so charming about a collapsed romance?
If minds are like parachutes, how best to keep them open?
Why do we take pleasure in reading obituaries?
What is the greatest trigger of dullness?
When are housewives desperate?
When should we bring hammer blows against the bell jar that protects dreamers from reality?
Name one universal rule of dressing for summer?
If your hubris was a dance, show me the first step.
What is the essence of suaveness?
What is the upside to depression?
What is the evolutionary purpose of feeling really sad?
In what way is chance a fool's name for fate?
Why all the questions?
How do you explain the allure of the night sky?
What is the best way to divest ourselves of a romantic object given by an ex?
Why are some kings obsessed with beheading their wives?
What is wrong with being trapped in the love space?
In what way is a room a second skin?
When should we recuse ourself?
What do animals not worry about going to heaven?
How can we keep the dogs at bay?
A little higher a little faster, easy to say but how do you do it?
What is the first piece of equipment you would install in a Seniors Playground?
When should we take our wigs off?
When do we need a Greek chorus?

What is the best training for life's cockpit?
Why is it time to ask smarter questions?
If how we spend our days is how we spend our lives, how do you spend your days?
In what way is reality only a convergence of multiple fantasies?
When is fun overrated?
Give an example of something that tastes as good as skinny feels?
What is it about families that is so scary?
Why are all the best people bonkers?
Who is to say what is proper?
Show me your smoulder.
When should we create our own world?
Why is that memories are all we are left with?
If you were to throw down some moves, what would you do?
Once we know, what should we do?
What are you going to do without your woman?
What do you do to mend a broken heart?
What *is* the same old story?
In what way are we all gurus now?
How do you get to your happy place?
Show me your signature move.
What happened to Superman?
What brings out your inner Goddess?
How far will 'cute' take you?
If love is a barcode, how do you read?
How do you know how far you can go?
What's in a brushstroke?
What are some good things about stalking?
In what way are men work?
Why does the trumpet sound so glorious?
Why did God make women so desirable?
Why are we suckers for love?
How can we make sure we wake up smarter than when we went to bed?
How can you work on not being unhappy?
What moves the human heart the most?
How can you garner the silent gratitude of history?
It is not too late for what?
What phrase would you like to ban from the English language?

Complete the following question. 'The hottest places in hell are reserved for ....'
If the best among us are in disguise, who is in disguise?
If you wanted to use a pseudonym, what would it be for?
If you can tell a Hapsburg by his jaw and a Kennedy by his incisors, how can you tell a WASP?
Complete the sentence. Banished from men's style should be tights, clashing tartans and ......
What sets off alarm bells on first dates?
What can you do if you are half a bubble off plumb?
Why does each generation imagine itself to be wiser than the one before?
How is love a dangerous disadvantage?
Why is more bewilderment better?
What does it mean when you don't like your friends?
What is the 51st way to leave a lover?
What sort of beauty does not threaten other women?
Why are men as we know them finished?
Why do men want to appear mysterious?
Why are actors so short?
Why are humans the only creatures that have hair instead of fur?
Why does beauty have trouble waking up?
How is confidence the ultimate fashion accessory?
Where is the real place where humans mistakenly believe they live?
Why the enduring appeal of bonnets, butlers and stiff upper lips?
How can you take control of the narrative?
What have you done to deserve the grand moniker 'I'?
What are the perils of online dating?
How are the stories we like to read like the lies we like to tell?
How can we avoid being too much Hamlet?
What do you really think about the male gaze?
Why should we chase the wind?
What is the essence of the art of smooze?
Why is it good to be cloistered?
How would you describe the interior lives of guys?
What about the crazy landscape of the fizzy and squish?
What's out there?
Why do women find 'tentative' so attractive in men?
How is genius just eternal patience?
What is the difference between the male gaze and female gaze?

How can you redirect the male gaze?
Explain why you would rather be invisible or travel in time.
If you met an alien from another planet, how would you explain the human condition?
How do you explain the hallucinatory character of the world?

Notes to explore questions

When do we earn our wisdom?
What we become often depends on what we learn at odd moments - wisdom comes at unexpected thresholds.

How would you like your portrait done?
What style of likeness would you like to be captured to represent who you really are? As old paint ages it sometimes becomes transparent and shows the original lines. This effect, when a painter changes course, is called 'pentimento' – an original conception is replaced by another. Just like life, one way of seeing, then seeing differently. That's my portrait.

What is the power of benign violation?
There is a theory that the secret to being funny is the same as the secret to being cool. And that secret is Benign Violation –the notion that the funniest punchline and the stylish behavior is the minor transgression – the low consequence breaking of useless rules. To be truly cool or funny means departing from the norms we consider unnecessary.

What is the power of negative thinking?

It is hard not to be skeptical of the cult of positive thinking, seems lightweight stuff in need of debunking from time to time. Does human happiness really depend on being positive at all times? Life has lots of bad bits that we have to accept with grace. We need a tough mindedness in the face of difficult circumstances. Happiness via positive thinking can be fleeting, while negative preparation generates a more dependable calm.

What makes us happy?
There is a debate about what make us happy. Is it a life of freedom and adventure, or a life that celebrates roots and connection? Research shows what the inner mind really wants is connection. Seems that happiness is not produced by conscious accomplishments. It is more a measure of how thickly the unconscious parts of our minds are intertwined with other people. Happiness seems to be determined by how much affection flows through us every day.

What new Superhero would you like to be?
Do you want to really fly? Repelling the earth with your body's anti—gravitons secretions? Or telekinetically control objects? Invisible and deflecting light beams with your eyes? Your 'nom de puissance' should reflect your extraordinariness. It should be a category killer. The first letter has to look impressive emblazoned on a leotard.

Why do we die?
We die because we were born. We were born because we are mortal. That's life.

Why is vapid so appealing?
Is beauty the wonder of wonders? Are outward appearances more intriguing than inner lives? Celebrities exhibit hidden depths of shallowness. All that publicity reduces them to a beautiful nothingness.

What is our attraction to unruly places?
It may seem obvious that we are local citizens first, and global citizens last. All our deadly disagreements can be reduced to either the protection or expansion of home. This ancient primacy of place, the human need for a '*genius loci*', despite our need to keep moving.

Although we live with the expectation that the world is fully visible and exhaustively known, we also need places that allow our thoughts to roam unimpeded. With so much of the world known, and that knowledge leading to control, we yearn for mystery, for another world within our world.

Where *does creativity come from?*
The idea of the solitary creator is a common feature of our cultural landscape. But is the lone genius a myth that has outlived its usefulness? Is a more accurate model emerging? The creative network as with the crowd–sourced Wikipedia or the writers' room seems more realistic. The real heart of creativity may be the intimate exchange of the creative pair.

How is the brain wired for the mature life?
A growing body of neuroscience research suggest that the human brain is wired for constant reinvention, not retirement. The mature brain may lose some of its processing speed and accuracy, but when challenged can keep growing and developing new strengths and assets. The younger brain cannot compete with the reservoirs of knowledge and wisdom that the mature brain carries.

What makes an inherently good observer?
When you are out of the main swim, you see what is going on?

Why are we attracted to ruins?
Ruins are the physical detritus of an earlier built life. Is it the leftover quality, the remains, that makes ruins so intriguing? Ruins represent both what has been lost and what can be reborn. After an interval of neglect, a discontinuity with the past, there is the possibility of renewal and starting again. I can't resist ruins, the more decrepit and forlorn, the more appealing. I fall in love with the abandonment and declaration of neglect. Let's face it everything, and everyone, is in some state of deterioration.

How long does it take to betray a secret?

A survey has revealed that women wait, on average, just over half an hour before betrayal. Men, on the other hand, are more strategic. Typically, they betray a secret to gain an advantage or trade information. Either way, best to keep our secrets to ourselves.

Why do we fear dragons?

Folklorists trace the dragon myth back to sources in ancient China, Rome, Greece and India and speculate that it had its genesis in the discovery of fossil bones from dinosaurs. Fables about winged, poison-spewing, fanged and clawed creatures combine a number of threats to ancient pre-human primates. Seems that our brain may be hardwired with an instinctive fear of dragons.

How can we use our body language to advantage?

Since we tend to interpret body language based on subconscious ideals, we can work on how we are viewed by others. We judge people's behaviour all the time and automatically assess whether they pose a danger or a benefit or are neutral. If we master the non-verbal clues we send, we can use body language to our advantage.

Research shows that words counts for a mere 7% of impact, tone for 38% and body language for 55%. That doesn't leave much wriggle room when our body cues are off.

How does the imagination shape reality?

The fundamental job of the imagination is to produce, out of the society we live in, a version of society we want to live in.

Why do we have this need for novelty?

It starts in infancy, with babies enraptured by novelty, and continues throughout our lives. It seems that human beings are 'neophiliacs'. We are wired by evolution for novelty, change and adaptation.

What is it about the male gaze?

The male gaze is supposed to be an exhilarating passage in the life of a woman. And then as women age and they don't care so much what men think of them, they are liberated from the tyranny of that male gaze. But does the mutual attraction of men for women and vice versa ever fade? The joys of flirtation do not have a defined shelf live. Being gazed upon, men or women, is not demeaning, it is empowering. It is what keeps all of us wanting to look good.

Why should we eliminate the gatekeepers?
By getting rid of the middle men, individuals become more directly empowered to launch their ideas. By seeding, nurturing, cultivating and executing your ambitions, there are no gatekeepers to turn you away.

What makes men happy?
The credit for growing old gracefully owes more to ourselves than our genetic makeup. Physical ageing after sixty is determined less by hereditary and more by habits formed prior to age fifty. Seems there might be a five-word conclusion to what makes men happy: *happiness is love.*

When they say 'prepare for Doomsday', what do they mean?
There was a prophecy not long ago, supposedly based on the Mayan calendar, that the world would end on December 21, 2012. Social media and Hollywood movies have indicated numerous ways the world might end. One danger might be a comet strike or a black hole. But Mankind may not need cosmic forces to bring on Armageddon. Nuclear war, global warming, or a disease pandemic could do the trick. Sun burnout is a sure thing, but not for another 4.5 billion years. Let's just get through another day.

How can we make sense of a life?
Does our society have a cultural bias towards career skills and is inarticulate when it comes to things that matter most? Intelligence and academic and career achievement may not correlate well with fulfillment. The traits that make a difference can't be taught in a classroom - the ability to inspire others, to read situations and discern underlying patterns, to build trusting relationships, to recognize and correct one's shortcomings, to imagine alternate futures

Brain science is illuminating the rich underwater where character is formed, and wisdom grows. A core finding of this work is that we are not primarily products of our conscious thinking. The conscious mind gives us one way of making sense of our environment. But the unconscious mind gives us other, more supple ways that emphasize the relative importance of emotion over pure reason, social connections over individual choice, moral intuition over abstract logic, perceptiveness over IQ. Living is inherently an emotional thing.

How do we earn our wisdom?
What we become often depends on what we learn at odd moments. Wisdom comes at unexpected thresholds.

How do we forgive?
Why is forgiveness so difficult and so necessary? Forgiveness is more than a spiritual thing – it is a means of promoting internal harmony. It's not for the person who hurts you. It's for you. Forgiveness is to move forward stronger.

How do we remember?
We know memory is a pliable thing. At best it is a dollar-store flashlight. Editing our memories is one of the ways we define ourselves. To curate our memories is to move forward.

What magic elixir would you like to create?
The powers we wished we had, the portions we could create. Part of the human imagination wants to live beyond our selves, to escape everyday living and cross to the kingdom of magic. The alchemist can change base metals into gold but our alchemy can be more exotic. Our transformation can be anything we want. A love potion? Youthful reincarnation? Or maybe just better hair?

How can you tell someone is lying?
You can argue that mendacity is part of modern life, a coping mechanism in a dog eat dog world of competition and ambition. Let's be honest: everybody lies or at least withholds the truth, in the interest of civility. How we might offend if we actually uttered the thoughts that arose in us. We can distinguish a continuum of lying with polite refrain at one end moving through charm and flattery, to manipulation and outright deceit and disinformation at the other end.
Knowing how to detect when someone is dancing on the lying continuum is an important life skill, a key determinant of Emotional Intelligence. They say the body never lies, hence the sweat, pulse and movement measurements on the lie detector test. Micro-expressions betray intent every time.

What is it about wild horses on the run?
Some visual moments can stop us in our tracks - a sight so uplifting or shocking that we are stunned by its awe. Wild horses on the run does it for me. To see a pack of horses at full gallop in their natural habitat is to give meaning to the myth that wherever Poseidon's trident struck the earth a horse appeared.
Sable Island is almost the last place on earth where a rowdy gang of horses can range at will away from civilization. There, a hundred miles off shore of Nova Scotia, framed by the purple of the ocean, the sapphire of the sky and the roar of the Atlantic surf, hundreds of wild horses run free, untamed and unbridled.

What is the secret to a successful long-distance relationship?
We know that relationships are hard work. The nature of a personal connection is to give, take, compromise and work out an equilibrium that is constantly shifting. It is a mystery what makes couples work. Every relationship has its own idiosyncratic dynamic.

In the type of world we live in with global and local being interchangeable, long distance affairs are not unusual, whether it be separate cities, counties or continents. Some argue that since absence makes the heart grow fonder, distance intensifies intimacy. We know that we can be miles apart in the same bed but if we are convinced of the naked singularity of our bond, we can make anything work.

How do our homes reflect who we are?
Our homes may represent the only haven we have in a world in which there is so little that we can control. Where we live become a retreat and sanctuary from the clutter on the other side of the threshold. When we shut the door, we leave the chaos behind.
We shape our dwelling and then our dwelling shape us. We surround ourselves with the artifacts of our life, talismans of our emotional and psychological journeys. We construct an environment of who we are, where we have been, and where we want to go.

Where is home?
Home is not just place. If we have to find home only in place, we will never find it. Let's face it no one is really where they started. Everyone is going somewhere. Place in and of itself doesn't have meaning. Home is where we find love and acceptance. Somewhere to bury our bones.

What is the essence of charm?
Charm, that holy grail of personality traits, appears as the gateway to a sophisticated life, a persona's elixir to winning friends and influencing people. As a way of dealing with people, charm will transport you to a lot of places.
Consider the elements of this winning trait, intelligence, humour, and wit combined with a sense of narrative. Understatement and self-effacement are also crucial. Well placed flattery can be effective. But an overdose or a too practiced style can have the opposite effect, turning charm into a tyranny of persuasion.
Charm can be a moveable trait, shining in different people at different times. The common denominator is a genuine curiosity in what the French call ' la condition humaine'. Charmers are fascinated with what makes people tick, good listeners and good talkers at the same time. We want to spend more time in their company because they make us feel good about ourselves, and who can't get enough of that.

What can you tell by how someone dances?

As an expression of who we are, dance is the choreography of our body language.

Everyone has a way of speaking to themselves through the coordination of their limbs. Ask anyone to demonstrate their 'happy dance' and you will get an infinite variety of movements, each an exposé of an individual psyche, and a peephole to an interior life.

People often surprise us by how they move, their rhythmic patterns of gestures revealing a part of their personality or a quirky font of body language. Some men don't like to dance because it puts them in uncomfortable territory. But ask guys to celebrate on the sports field and you will see all manner of cavorting.

As a form of identification, dance is the equivalent of a finger imprint or an iris scan. Immigration officers should ask us for our signature move.

What is the best way to put down roots?

There is a universal yearning for somewhere to call home, somewhere we feel secure. But we move around so much. With all our anxieties and ambitions, we never stay still. We are a restless sort, wanting to travel and discover all parts of our world. No one is where they started from, relocating within one or several generations.

Mobility is unsettling. How can we reconcile the basic need to root and grow in a community, with the equally strong need for exploration and new beginnings? What is the secret of feeling at home? Is it where we find love and security? Employment? Or is it where we find peace and acceptance, good soil to bury our bones?

Why do we yearn for an identical twin?

Some believe that we all start out in the womb as a zygote that splits in half but rarely do both survive. We begin life's journey craving our other half. We feel incomplete, something is missing, our sibling has gone AWOL. An emotional vacuum has been created by the missing divided embryo.

This business of identical twins is a curious matter. Like alter egos and genetic clones, one cannot twitch without the other tugging. Soul mates and womb mates, identical twins mirror each other in a DNA marvel. It is a common fantasy that any one of us may have a clone, not only a human mirror but an ideal companion, someone who understands us perfectly.

Better to have a fraternal twin, two separate eggs fertilized by different sperm at the same time. A brother, a sister, a life-long chum of the exact age instead of a womb mate who sabotages our sense of personal uniqueness.

What would Saitarg say?

At the moment of decision when time has expired and we must move on, that tipping point known to the French as ' le moment juste', wouldn't we like to have a private muse, someone to tell us what to do, or nudge us in a direction. Our kingdom for a Confucius to keep us on the moral high ground and maintain a compass to our conscience.

The path to the high road is littered with barriers. It is hard to navigate such obstacles as greed, jealousy, revenge and lust? That sage, our bespoke savant who has grappled with the philosophical issues and has learned from millennia of behaviour, can take us by the hand and show us the way.

Saitarg is the reference figure for me. He has accumulated great deposits of natural wisdom and insight. He knows how to mine those reserves, the indispensable 'savoir faire' of life experience.

What is the key to being the perfect house guest?

Although much is accessible as a tourist, how much better to be invited as a guest, a privileged lodger at the home of the estate owner where we can enjoy the ambience under the tutelage of the proprietor. Why is that only a few get invited again and again to attend the private retreats of mere acquaintances while others can scarce summons an invitation from next of kin?

There are rules of engagement and a code of conduct born through generations of practice at the country houses of the European gentry. The standard etiquette is well known - the arrival with bags of imported foods, house gifts, and more drink than you consume. The participation in the rituals of the family, no matter how disinclined you are. The availability to cheerfully help with the chores and property maintenance.

The single most important encyclical of being the perfect house guest is to observe the natural domestic rhythms. Hosts enjoy public times and private spaces. Know when to disappear and be quiet, when to engage and amuse. Your job is to enhance the conviviality of the hearth, to fill the proprietors with the glow of their achievements and then depart midst protests and a thirst for more of your charms.

Why should we dance more?

We know dance to be a universal language of self-expression, a signature way of communicating with ourselves and to others. We each have a way of following our inner voice in an orchestration of motion. We move our body and limbs to our own natural rhythms

Admittedly dancing does not pay the rent or put out the garbage, but it does elevate our spirits. The blood starts to flow, happy in the moment as we indulge the spirit of the now. Dance is free, can be done anywhere, and connects to our deepest psyche.

We may not have Michael Jackson's slide or Fred Astaire's glide but we can still jump with joy, wag our head and spin round and round. We just need to get out there and move. Strut and boogie, snap and pop, and see how good it feels.

What would Roger do?

At the moment of crisis, when the adrenalin flows at the call to action, when extraordinary things are expected of ordinary people, what to do? Instinct takes hold as our inner self is actualized. Quick thinking can salvage a situation. If only someone could guide us on the right thing to do.

We need a reference, someone to call on to direct our hand. In the movies and comic books it might be Superman, or Spiderman, or an Avatar. In real life it is our gut feeling or training that mobilizes us, recognizing the greater the uncertainly and the longer the prevarication, the less timely the intervention.
Roger is my reference point. She is my ten-year old Collie-Shepherd mix, who has the proper instincts at the decisive moment. She is guardian of the homestead who knows who is welcome and who to keep at bay. She is always working, monitoring the perimeters, plunging into crevices, averting danger and disaster. At the moment of crisis, Roger is my beacon.

Why do we like boundaries so much?
In life we need markers. Boundaries define our property, our behavior and our conscience by informing what belongs to us, what is acceptable and legal and ethical according to the moral standards and the laws of our group. Imagine the chaos, the ruthlessness, the incivility that would be let loose in a society without boundaries.
Whether a line in the sand, a steel enclosure or a codified set of laws, boundaries tell us where we belong, and how to behave in relation to others in our community. As a reference point boundaries provide guidance for a journey. It is not so much that we like them, but we need them.

Name one habit of civilized living.
Why do we fall prey to the notion of civilized living, a lifestyle connecting us to a history of genteel antecedents? Is it a pretension to believe that we have to keep up standards? We like to have assurance we are living a certain quality of life. These become markers of comfort befitting a civilized world.
There is a reason that habit is called the flywheel of society, it's most valuable conserving agent. We hold on to certain rituals that persuade us we are living according to our expectation. Habit is what keeps us going. It is like a thread that we weave every day until it cannot be broken, or the buoy of navigation that gives us the confidence we are on a good course.

I do insist on a cocktail at sundown, changing for dinner, lingering over good fare, and conversation. I can't image getting through a day without skipping rope or standing on my head. But more than anything else, laughter is my civilizing habits, the search for the light side.

What is the essence of charisma?

Charisma is thought of as the motherlode of personality traits, the elusive amalgam of qualities that we aspire to but few possess. We are not sure exactly what it is, or how it manifests itself, except that we all feel we know charisma when we meet it. Charisma is not something that can be observed in the frontal cortex lobe of a brain scan. You either have it or you don't, and most people don't

Charisma is associated with superior beings, those who are wayfinders, who leap across the chasm, who know the way. The essence of charisma is in the ability to inspire hope. Someone to show us the way. Let's face it there is a little part of the lost soul in each of us. Sometimes we just cannot get it right on our own.

Why is it a curse to be too good looking?

If contemporary society venerates anything, it is beauty. We need to feel we are good looking or least attractive and not out of the norm. In a society that seems fixated on fashion and appearances, we want to feel good about how we present to others. Confidence comes from a positive awareness of how we show. Plain or ordinary is okay but too good looking? Instinctively you want to file this query under "are you kidding me"?

There has been research galore on the notion of the ideal proportions of the face and the body with mountains of evidence to suggest that certain ratios and a strong nose and chin line with bone structure to suit reads well. But good looks a curse? Reflect on the fate of Narcissus, the Greek demi-god who was so entranced by his own beauty that he killed himself. Or the case of Dorian Gray who was so besotted by his own beauty that he entered into a Faustian contract with the Devil.

If there is real substance behind the uber good looks, chances are you won't be taken seriously. Too good looking is interpreted as superficial. Convention says a woman has to ignore her looks to be taken seriously. Good looks can become a crutch on which you rely instead of putting in those thirty thousand hours of hard work. If beauty is in the eye of the beholder, this is one curse we can do without.

What sort of space gives you the shivers?
Have you experienced a frisson when you enter a wonderful physical place? A space that speaks to your core being. Our build environment can trigger a kind of exhilaration in those who are sensitive to architecture. For me it is not the grandeur of the space but the intimacy of corners, the opportunity for the imagination to soar and a feeling I have to return.

How does pleasure work?
How can we explain why we like what we like? Is there a grand unifying explanation? Is there a pleasure centre in the brain which lights up at all our indulgences?
Like taste in art, we know what we like and don't like without understanding why. Unifying principles are tenuous because pleasure basically works individually, springing from a mixture of experience, context, physiology and biology. The important thing is the experience, the four hundred thread count Egyptian cotton sheets, the double expresso, the ultra-dry martini. It doesn't matt
er how it works, it's the glow of satisfaction that counts.

How does philosophy play a role in everyday life?
The everyday is 99 per cent of our lives. Back in Socrates' time philosophy promoted itself as a guide to the good life, but today it seems preoccupied with the remaining 1 per cent. In the school of life, philosophy can still play a role if we just examine our daily routine.

The word 'philosophy' means 'the love of wisdom' which is a practical art aimed at making deft judgments in the midst of everyday complications. In this sense philosophy is about recognizing the ambiguity of life as it is lived. Socrates would be just as interested in how much to tip the waiter as in whether God exists. If we don't think about the everyday while we live it, there is not going to much time left over for reflection

Why is religion everywhere?

The persistence of religious systems throughout human history must mean that there is something in religion that satisfies the most basic yearnings of human beings.

Since the brain defines who we are, and it is more comfortable believing than doubting, the human mind could be God's chosen instrument. If there is a neuroscience of devotion, perhaps we can understand the prevalence of religion because it simply comforts us. The strongest argument for religion is not that it puts us in touch with God, but that it puts us in touch with each other.

Why should we seek enlightenment for everyone?

Most people work primarily to solve their own problems. It is part of the human journey to seek some sort of enlightenment for ourselves. We hope this translates into serenity in our lives and an appreciation of our place in the world. But what if we were to enlarge our compassion and seek enlightenment for everyone. Tibetan Buddhism embraces all sentient beings. Wouldn't be good to live in a world that embraces selflessness? There is too much misery and too many hellish places on earth where evil thrives.

How do you account for wisdom?

For all the palaver of wisdom, the distillation of life experiences that is supposed to bring us serenity, clear-headedness may simply be a function of the brain slowing down. Research shows that with aging, wisdom is the result of a decrease in impulsivity. Older people are less likely to respond thoughtlessly to negative emotional stimuli because their brains have slowed down compared to younger people. The elder brain is less dopamine dependent, making people less emotional and more sage.

What is so menacing about orthodoxy?
Orthodoxy, the holding of correct, conventional and currently acceptable beliefs, is dangerous because it means not thinking. Orthodoxy is unconsciousness.

If you believed in the end of the world, what might be the signs it is coming?
Those who believe in the end of the world also believe that there will be signs that it is coming. Natural disasters, such as major earthquakes and fires, bring spikes of apocalyptic forecasts. There are evangelical Christian websites that feature a regularly updated 'rapture index' that gauges the imminent approach of the world's end. The Rapture Index is a sort of Dow Jones for end-time activity. This prophetic speedometer includes many phenomena that we accept as part of the modern condition – wild weather, economic hardship, debt, and drought. Should we fasten our seatbelts?

Give an example of an unanswerable question.
They say it is more important to ask the right question than give the right answer. The Socratic Method of questioning leads to self-awareness and enlightenment. The Buddhists understand the power of an open question that can lead to clarity. But some questions are really tough. The website 'Ask Jeeves' has compiled what is calls the top 10 "unanswerables" which include such stumpers as "what is the meaning of life?", "what is love?" and "what is the secret to happiness?"
All I want to know is how long will I live.

What is the best thing you have ever found?
The serendipity of coming across an unexpected treasure is one of life's pleasures. Sometimes the best surprises come in small packages like a shoebox – letters, photos, cards and keepsakes that bring back memories. Or a portrait at garage sale that turns out to be valuable. A stone or shell on a beach that adorns the mantle above the hearth to evoke the best vacation you ever had.

What is the essence of a good swagger?
There is nothing like a good swagger to get attention but how do we get to be 'swaggerific'- the amble that drives our fans into a frenzy? Swagger derives from swag which began life in the Middle Ages as a bulging bag. The unwieldy nature of the bulging bag led to swag as a verb meaning to sway. The essence of a good swagger is to put yourself on parade with an overweening confidence. The physiology is important – assume the alpha posture. You have to practice or hire a swagger coach. Okay let's see your stuff.

What is the essence of suave?
Suave derives from the Latin *suavis* meaning sweet and pleasant, and can be traced back further to the Indo-European base *suad* . From *suad* the Greeks got *hedon*, pleasure, the source of our hedonism. Over time suave evolved from sweet and agreeable to charming, urbane and sophisticated. In a texting world suave is up for grabs, morphing into a feeling, an inspiration, and a style. Suave is radically cool. It is what makes you calm and think clearer than your enemies.

How are you going to handle the first mobile meltdown?
A single YouTube viewing consumes nearly 100 times as much cellular bandwidth as a voice call. Your connection to YouTube might be the first to go on the day of the first mobile meltdown. Twitterspace will also be down. Your email is stalled as the world's phone networks come crashing down.

Some sort of collapse is a real possibility. Cellular networks are showing signs of strain especially in big cities. The only way out may be to connect with real people in real time.

Why are men disposable?
Men die 5.2 years younger than women, spend their last decade in worse health and die earlier of all the leading causes of death. The reason women live longer than men – and why the final act of sex discrimination favours females over males – may have a scientifically valid explanation. There is growing evidence to suggest that men are literally more disposable than woman because the cells of their bodies are not genetically programmed to last as long as they are in females. The notion that women are less disposable than men makes excellent biological sense. The mater is ground zero of species continuity. One man and three hundred women can keep a civilization going.

What is the best way to decode a smile?
From childhood on we are told it is our duty to smile, part of our learned social graces. Happiness is not the cause of all smiles. The smile is the default position of those who like politicians want to exude confidence as is the red-carpet grin of celebrities conveying the utter marvelousness of their closely observed lives.
Long ago in our evolution humans developed the 'voluntary' as well as the 'involuntary smile.' The intentional or fake smile is designed to seduce and charm. A genuine smile begins in the eyes, slips on slowly and doesn't last long. It is the fresh happiness of an honest emotion.

Why are fairy tales immortal?
Why have fairy tales not fizzled away to the domain of kiddy literature? Everywhere you turn the fairy tale is flourishing. The human disposition for narrative and the possibilities for change continue to fascinate. Although many fairy tales are utopian, they unsettle us by showing what we lack and how we might compensate. Fairy tales hint of happiness, often illuminating ways into the future. They expose and resolve deep rooted moral conflicts. Fairy tales teach us we are all misfit for the world and yet somehow, we all fit together.

Why is silence golden?

Why is noise winning and silence becoming a novelty? The word 'noise' comes from the Latin 'nausea' as in disgust. We know that excessive noise is stressful. Hearing loss is a chronic condition in North America. Seems that a lot of people think that to be loud is to be alive, and making noise is a way for the powerless to assert their presence.
If silence is becoming rare, why can't we bring back more quiet places, patches of undeveloped land, riverbanks, and cemeteries. Cities need acoustical contrasts. There is wisdom in silence, if not rapture. Silence quells the internal chaos, soothing the irritation of lives in constant motion. Silence takes us beyond ourselves, to connection and authenticity.

What is the essence of sophistication?
What we now think of chic has never entirely lost its early negative associations.

At some point the word 'sophistication' transitioned from being a derogatory term to something to celebrate. Originating from the ancient Greek word for wisdom, sophistication has evolved from being defined as 'adulteration' in the 1799 edition of Samuel Johnson's *Dictionary*. Today it is a more diffuse concept applying to everything stylish, luxurious, or technically complex.
Unlike trendiness, sophistication involves cool – the ability to intuit dress and style codes. A key to the modern interpretation is the involvement of taste, elegance and refinement. There can be no sophistication without discrimination. *You* have to choose.

Why the eternal allure of procrastination?
Procrastination – it's irrational, inefficient and self-destructive. So why do we all do it? Delay is part of the human condition. Goofing off is fun.
If we could identify the main source of why we put things off, perhaps we could prevent it. Although there are several predictive personality traits, one stands out above the rest. The Achilles heel of procrastination turns out to be impulsiveness – living impatiently in the moment and wanting it all now.

But the upside is that impulsive procrastinators tend to have more energy in the crunch. They have more ability to focus than most people. They get in the zone in a burst of creative energy.

What is the secret to the ability to fascinate others?
How is it that some people have an ability to bewitch? Competition for the brief window onto our consciousness is driving advertisers into a frenzy. In the art of persuasion, fascination elevates the credibility of you and your message.
There seem to be triggers to successful persuasion and captivation. An appeal to things like lust, mystique, alarm and trust are rooted in human biology. We just have to figure out to activate them.

What is the best way to take pain out of memory?
All of us are shaped by life's experiences.

The brain has a remarkable capacity for keeping track of our past experiences which can be more of a curse than a blessing if those memories are painful. We want to forget traumas. It seems that we can exert some control of what gets in and stays in long term memory. This episodic memory is largely determined by what we are focused on. By focusing on the non-emotional details of a painful memory, we can grow, learn and adapt.
How are you able to resist temptation?
We all experience the tug of war between willpower and temptation. People tend to overestimate their ability to resist temptations around them. They have this self-control hubris, they believe the can handle more than they can.

Show me your waggle dance.

We humans should pay more attention to the functioning of the bee hive. Worker bees have the important job of letting their hive mates know where to find food. They pass on the information by performing a 'waggle dance' containing coded directions to nectar-rich flowers. Now show me where I can find that killer latte.

What determines a sense of fulfillment in life?
We are not primarily the product of conscious thinking. The conscious mind gives us one way of making sense of our environment. But the unconscious mind gives us other. The cognitive revolution of the past thirty years provides a different perspective on our lives: one that emphasizes the relative importance of emotion over reason, social connections over individual choice, moral intuition over abstract logic, perceptiveness over IQ.
It allows us to tell a different sort of success story, an inner story to go along with the conventional surface one. It makes a distinction between mental strength, the processing power of the brain, and mental character, the virtues that lead to practical wisdom. In the debate about what really makes us happy, there is a shift away from freedom and adventure to a celebration of roots and connection.

Why should we outsource our love life?
Internet dating has introduced a new stress to the world of finding romantic connections. The pictures, the preferences, the interminable list of hobbies and childhood memories, sifting through hundreds of online profiles can be exhausting work.
But relief is in sight, Thanks to the arrival of online 'dating concierges', overwhelmed singles can hand the job over to a third party who, for a fee, will do the heavy lifting. Dating consultants will create your web profile, plan the date, down to the clothes you wear and the place you go for dinner.

How do you know you are about to have an epiphany??

Epiphany is that moment of clarity when the inner light bulb switches on. It is a revelation, a tipping point that changes everything. We all want to have one, the more the better on the road to self-awareness. They help in figuring out how life works.
You have to love the word – epiphany- the luscious way it rolls off the tongue like a pomegranate seed tumbling into a salad. It has sexy Greek and Latin antecedents with hip biblical references. But how do we know we are in that moment of awakening? When I feel the shiver, I lie down so that I can give birth to the epiphany slowly and work through the fresh insight.

What is the trick to being on time?
Some people make a habit of running late. You might be a pleaser and an over doer, packing in too much. Or maybe you think your time is more valuable than the time of those who are waiting. Either way you need some time-management skills. Don't say yes right away. Learn how to say no. Be realistic about how long things take. Practice getting there early. Relax and zone down, no more shame about pulling up late.

Why are humans so smelly?
Pungent body odour from sweating adult human skin is unique in the animal kingdom. Humans turn out to be particularly smelly because odours are released from nearly every part of our bodies. While we tend to think of other animals as smelling more unpleasantly than we do, other mammals have significantly fewer volatile compounds emanating from their skin.

Why should we treat ourselves as well as we treat our friends?
How people view themselves is the basis for a burgeoning new area of research called 'self-compassion' – how kindly we treat ourselves. It turns out that people who find it easy to be supportive and understanding to others score low on self-compassion tests. They beat themselves up for perceived failures like being overweight or not exercising. Giving ourselves a break and accepting our imperfections is the first step to better health. High self-compassion means less depression and more optimism. Now that we are happier maybe we can lose some weight.

What is your cocktail manifesto?

At some level we all have a preference, if not a philosophy, for the cocktail. If I had to set down the law, I would banish all mixed drinks. Public enemy #1 is rum because rum requires fruit juice, poison to my type of cocktail.
In my books the cocktail universe shrinks to two choices: scotch or a martini. The martini can be shaken or stirred, with olives, a twist of lemon or a drop of lemon oil. But it must remain as dry as the desert with only a whiff of vermouth. The cocktail hour is the magic moment, the hour of hush and wonder when affections glow and valour is reborn.

How does the internet disconnect us from each other?
I thought we looked to social media to defend us against loneliness. By being alone together we expect more from technology and less from each other. Digital natives use the mobile internet to manage their relationships, expecting a response shallow and fast
When it is 'I share, therefore I am', we are using others to prop ourselves up. We are using public space to be alone with our personal networks. In online intimacies we hope for compassion but often get the cruelty of strangers. Without connecting with real people in real time, we never get to figure out meaning.

What is the power of daydreaming?
Can daydreaming, that ubiquitous human pastime, have benefits? Research has shown that our minds wonder almost half of our waking hours but not all types of mental wonderings are good. Being able to escape the monotony of rote work is not necessarily a gift though it may bring relief to those who can sustain a rich imaginary life.
You are better off focusing on what you are doing than entertaining pleasurable fantasies. But there does appear to be a link between a certain style of daydreaming and creative problem solving. If you want your daydreams to be productive, keep track of your thoughts. But if you want to be happy, be here now.

Why does hierarchy matter?

A funny word that 'hierarchy' with its Latin and Greek antecedents referring to the rule of the high priest. Why do we humans thrive on a sense of order and rely on it? It seems that having a clear standing makes us feel more comfortable, more productive and happier. Could it be that having a taste for rank is a key part of what makes us a successful social species?

What is the single most defining element of a human culture?
What is this thing called 'culture'? Is it a useful organizing principle to understand distinct social communities distinguished by language and adaptive inclination? Culture is the acknowledgement of the unique and ever–changing constellation of how we live and what we aspire to. Culture springs from a spirit of promise, and a *visionary wisdom* that is always at risk.

How do you know your network is getting too big?
Networking, we are told, is the key to getting ahead. It is who you know as much as what you can do, that will shape your career and successes. But is networking all it's cracked up to be?
Virtual friends have to be managed, fed information, photos and tidbits to remind them why they are part of your community and worth following. Virtual friends take time and focus. Might be better to retreat back to the old fashion notion of friends as real people in real time? The handful who you are really connected to. The kind who have shared experiences and emotions with you. Aren't they the ones who will hold your hand through the rough patches, tweets and blogs be damned?

What is the best way to deal with unrequited love?
The slow burn of unrequited love has a long and glorious history in literature and in life: Dante's love for Beatrice in The Divine Comedy; Charlie Brown's infatuation with the Red-Haired Girl in Peanuts. Unless you enjoy being a martyr or relish torture of the mind, it is so much healthier to enjoy reciprocated passion.
One of pop's greatest ballads provides a useful strategy. The key lyric goes like this: "If you can't be with the one you love, love the one you're with." Nothing better assuages the pain of love denied than high voltage body heat from a more receptive partner.

What does it mean to be a prisoner of freedom?

If freedom is what life's work is all about, the end game of our toils and contributions, how do we become enslaved by its elixir? Or is freedom just another word for nothing left to lose? Can a surfeit of options lead to inertia, confusion and a longing for less choice?

How did you get so lucky?
Why is it that luck, Lady Luck, is seen as feminine? Perhaps that great leveler to which we all aspire lacks a manly swagger because luck is just a fool's name for fate. And Destiny like karma is always Her. Is the chanciness of being lucky completely random? Or can luck be made more rational by having a PMA (a positive mental attitude), and an eye cocked for opportunity? Toil and sweat might just be the birth mother of Good Fortune.

How do you use your wriggle room?
A wriggler – we all recognize the movements – the squirming, the slithers, the squiggles. Also known as the slack to maneuver, a breather to get out of trouble. Or like a mulligan in golf, a chance to replay the shot. All of us, at one time or another, have felt 'boxed' in. Stuck in one of life's cul de sacs with a nasty bit of business hovering into view.
Such moments are the time to focus on that indispensable concept- *wriggle room* – the margin to escape a dark hole. Wriggle room is our salvation in tight corners, those little stratagems that buy us time. Sometimes it requires a little artful dissemblance. Other times it involves going AWOL until emotions simmer down. Often 'fessing up' with some old- fashioned remorse. Appropriate word-smithery and ' mea culpas' are helpful. Wriggle room, no home should be without one.

When is love not enough?
If we were devoted to North American culture, we might be led to think that love, hopeless romantic love, head over heels stuff, would get us through anything. In the movies love is life's ultimate elixir. The romantic myth is that love is the miracle cure, and when partnered with our soul mate, we can conquer all.
But is love ever enough? Or is it something that happens to two people who don't know each other. We know how the hottest love can have the coldest end. Is love enough in hard times and sick times? in war and across time zones? Self- love, resourcefulness and wisdom should not be underrated in the calculus of survival.

When should we be skeptical?
There are some personality traits or skill sets that equip us better than others for survival. One thinks of emotional intelligence and common sense. Practicality also takes us a long way. Included in the front ranks of these forearming tools is skepticism, the ability to withhold or suspend belief until there is more evidence.
Though skeptics, like cynics, often get a bad rap, they are fundamental to the sound functioning of society. It is prudent to assume a healthy skepticism toward pretty well everything. Above all we need to beware the Big Truths, questioning, doubting, watching. A measure of doubt is world suffocating in hype and sizzle leads to our own self-discovery.

What does it take to reveal who you really are?
Many people hide behind a mask and present themselves to the world not as who they are but as who they would like to be. Most of us spend a little part of each day avoiding the reality of our lives, maybe just by escaping to a movie or settling into a romance novel. Each of us builds our own path to self-awareness, a personal approach to the understanding of who we are.
Often an external stimulus or extraordinary intervention is required to reach the truth. A martini, a joint, the comfort of old friends, the sudden face of illness, a transcendental experience all can accelerate the moment of awakening when protective layers are dropped. Sometimes we just have to stop editing our lives. We need to get out of our own way.

Why do we like surfaces so much?
Surface and superficial seem interchangeable, both derogatory and shallow. Surface rules in fashion, conversation, media and even ethics. What is not to like about surfaces? They are easy to reach, attractive on the eye, undemanding of time and best of all, allow us to rest and not penetrate deeper. Surface is a well-worn path.

What might we find if we plumb the depths? Do we want to expose the discrepancies between the outside and the inside? The protective husk and the vulnerable core? To many people their surfaces are their depths. Surface is all many of us will ever have but with it comes patina, that well-worn countenance of time. Let's indulge the glitter, the sizzle and the touch? Not many can cope with a more profound truth. There is nothing wrong with gliding effortlessly on top.

Who is riding in your sidecar?
Is there a better way to enjoy a crisp morning than bundled up in a sidecar of a Ural Patrol motorcycle zigzagging through a forest of fall colours. Who do you want to have as companion riding in your sidecar to share the exhilaration? Who do you want to see through your goggles, when drunk with wind in your mouth, and the unexpected vista around the next corner, you look over at your fellow traveler with a knowing glance?
For me the choice is obvious, a loyal friend, an outstanding sleuth and swashbuckler, my dog Roger. Outfitted in a leather helmet and a cape lashing behind her, she leans into the weather, awaiting her next assignment.

When did you last feel transported?
The idea is seductive - escaping everyday life, slipping away from the monotony of our routines and the drab regularity of our rituals. We need patterns and anchors but crave freedom and adventure. Unless we are able to get away from the beast of our reality, we may be condemned to living it.
Some need excitement and the aura of possibility more than others. Some prefer to stay close to home, others to travel great distances to find their otherworldliness and access their magic kingdoms.

Who is the stranger at your door?
A beguiling concept this notion of a 'stranger', an outsider who tries to connect with your world. The newcomer can be welcomed as a harbinger of good things to come or shunned as a destabilizer who comes to wreak havoc. Opening doors to strangers is a way of inviting change but why rustle the nest?

Should we open doors to the unknown? We may not want intrusions but imagine the possibilities if we do open the door. A conversation with a shape shifter, the possibility of falling in love. The announcement of a lottery winner followed by a happy dance. I long to greet someone for the first time and make a connection that will change my life. We would turn on the threshold and leave everything behind.

What do you wish your mother understood about you?
We should not confuse the unconditional love of a parent with an understanding of who we are. Some parents find it difficult to accept that their offspring are not clones of themselves. In term of genetic structures and psychological profiles, children are unique composites. Which can lead to something short of complete parental insight into what makes us tick.
We know how Mum or Dad can impose their agendas, trying to make us what they want us to be or could not be themselves. Their dreams for us can become our nightmares. Wouldn't it better if every child was made to feel they could do anything and then left alone to find their own way

Give an example of a universal truth?
When doubt is the stem cell of our culture, why search for certainty, the bitch goddess of our needs? What if it is all about random choice in a universe of chaos? To give meaning to our lives, we search for patterns to hang onto. We need faith that there are governing principles of our existence. To qualify as a universal truth, we have to deal with reality across all spectrums of race, culture and time. For example *'It can always get worse.'*

Take a universal aspect of human existence – food. Is there a truth about how much we need to eat. *'The less you eat, the longer you live.'* What about *'the need to believe in something larger than ourselves'.* Or a moral position. *'It is always better to take the high road.'* Or the need for emotional connection, *''love makes the world go round'.* For me it is enough to make it through each day putting one foot ahead of the other, universal truths be damned.

What makes a successful dinner party?

A dinner party is a signature of a certain quality of life. By bringing together family and friends and sometimes strangers in an intimate atmosphere, we share food, drink and our sense of joie de vivre. By inviting others into our home, our safe space, we are saying 'we like you, we want to get to know you better'.

Why are some so much better than others? Good food and grog are overrated. What counts are the people, the chemistry of the invitees, the conversation, the ambience and above all the sense of inclusion.

We may need little tricks to cross the barrier from formal to fun. We use New Yorker cartoons to indicate the seating plan, and then welcome friends in a form of grace that recognizes each individual. I invite guests to give spontaneous testimony, occasionally being rewarded with a perfect limerick. In the end it is the accessibility of the hosts that gives a dinner party a life of its own.

What is the secret to staying fabulous?

There is something about the state of 'fabulousness' that is so over the top, it is appealing. Part of the hyperbole in the world of fashion and style where overstatement and flattery are expected. The idea that the rest of us can have the qualities of being 'fabulous' is intoxicating.

We don't want to peak too soon. We want to look forward to getting if not faster and stronger, than wiser and funnier. Our sense of worth is governed by feelings of confidence and well -being. We have to figure out the things that make us happy each day. Might be a midnight picnic, a martini in the bathtub or shopping for shoes. I have evolved my own regime to maintain personal vigor, a set of encyclicals that keeps me striving for the 'fabulous' benchmark. I don't expect everyone to skip rope, stand on their head, and make every decision in fifteen seconds, but it keeps me on track of that superlative goal.

Why do we love our pets so much?
How can we explain the deep emotional attachments we develop with our pets? For the most part animals are better companions than humans because they tend not to use the word 'relationship'.

They do not sulk, or stop taking calls. We are not just talking cats and dogs, but any type of domesticated creature. A friend has a dancing cockatoo who boogies to the infectious beat of ABBA.
I am convinced that animals like humans, possess nuanced moral systems. I love my Roger, a shepherd/collie mix, for her intelligence and communication skills. As a first-rate swashbuckler and sleuth, there is no mission I can't send her on. I only wish I was half the person Roger thinks I am.

How can we give fate a twist?
Science has taught us that instead of being pre-destined by the Fates, stuff just happens. Good and bad. The universe is a cold random place and we are just bits of assembled carbon. I'd like to return to the quaint old-fashioned idea of destiny when the gods could not resist meddling in our lives. I want the gods to come out of retirement and start fooling with my life but only in a good way.

How can you be an evangelist for happiness?

With happiness as the holy grail for ageing boomers, the question becomes how we get there. Who will be our evangelist in the art of feeling good? Someone with cordial charm and socially inclusive who is immune to solemnity. Pleasure is a serious matter. Glumness is self-defeating. If we insist on bliss and lightness, we must accept the mood doesn't last.

What about the power of aphrodisiacs?
Is there really such a thing as an aphrodisiac? Can a particular food manipulate our sexual desire? Aphrodisiacs have been used for thousands of years around the world but is there science behind the claims? Some foods may make people more relaxed or more happy but sexual desire is a complicated business.
It seems that there are some foods that can double as an aphrodisiac. Scientific literature indicates that ginseng and saffron increase sexual desire as does yohimbine found naturally in trees grown in West Africa. Cloves, garlic and ginger have good success. But we need to find more ingredients that can serve as alternative to Viagra and Cialis. And not chocolate and alcohol.

How does happiness attain you?
It is said that happiness is like the watched pot that never boils. Like chasing a butterfly, the more you chase it, the more it eludes you. But if you turn your attention to other things, it comes and sits softly on your shoulder.

What is the purpose of writing your own story?
It is said that telling a story, helps you discover what the story is. In that sense by writing your tale you learn what that story means to you. You are doing more that writing what you know, you are writing what you imagine you know. The power of your words can move the human heart and create a better world.

What are we going to do with all this information?

The problem with information is that there is always too much of it. Because information is a measure of quantity not meaning, communication takes place all the time without human input. If information can spread in ways that have nothing to do with human intentions or desires, humans have ceased to be in control of circuits of communications. Does that mean that a world of boundless information is a world of endless possibilities?

What does a smile mean?
There is a view that certain emotions are biologically basic. Psychologists support the notion that all humans have the same set of biological emotions so that people scowl only when they are angry or pout only when they are sad. The commonly held belief is that certain facial expressions evolved to express certain mental states. But isn't there a tremendous variety in what bodies and people do in anger, or sadness or in fear. People do a lot of things when they are upset. Sometimes they yell, sometimes they smile.

What is the most important component of happiness?
The World Happiness Report, commissioned for the United Nations Conference on Happiness, concludes that the Danes are the happiest people on Earth. Apparently Danes find their national identity in a quality called *hygge*, often translated as 'coziness' – something distinct from *joie de vivre*.
Although the authors understand the utilitarian view that happiness is the sum of momentary pleasures, misery the sum of momentary pains, they favour the longer-term, retrospective view because it influences future decisions. The truth is that happiness is multidimensional. It cannot be measured on a single scale. Money isn't everything, but *hygge* isn't everything either – not even in dark Scandinavian winters.

Why do people cheat?
Everyone has the capacity to be dishonest, and almost everyone cheats – just a little.

What is it about the search for glory?

Glory seems to be a discredited word, spoiled perhaps by a too close association with military grandeur. It has been hijacked by fame and ambition. True glory is a private and discreet virtue and only fully realized in solitariness.

Why does architecture matter?
Most people have good instincts about architecture. They have an instant reaction to a building. Architecture begins to matter when it prods our imagination and pokes our emotions. It makes a connection with our core being, whether it be awe, or delight or perplexity. Even the thrill of the unexpected. Architecture brings a visceral understanding of space and how we fit into it.

What is the secret to success?
One word, a character trait, unrelated to IQ, and that word is 'grit'. Grit means perseverance zeal, controlled effort and stamina. Learn it. Practice it.

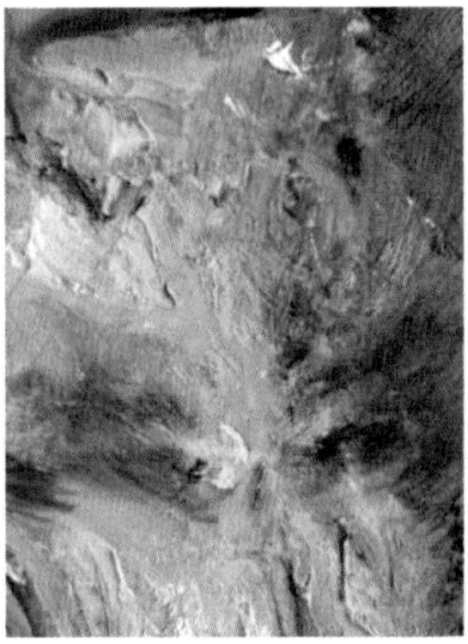

Go Quest

48294117R00055

Made in the USA
Middletown, DE
13 June 2019